THE SEEDS
OF LOVE

THE SEEDS OF LOVE

GROWING MINDFUL RELATIONSHIPS

by **Jerry Braza**

TUTTLE Publishing
Tokyo | Rutland, Vermont | Singapore

Published by Tuttle Publishing, an imprint of Periplus Editions (HK) Ltd.

www.tuttlepublishing.com

Copyright © 2011 Jerry Braza

Library of Congress Cataloging-in-Publication Data
Braza, Jerry.
The seeds of love : growing mindful relationships / by Jerry Braza.
  p. cm.
Includes bibliographical references.
ISBN 978-0-8048-4169-6 (pbk.)
1. Consciousness. 2. Attention. 3. Love. 4. Interpersonal relations. I. Title.
BF311.B7158 2011   158.2--dc22

                    2011012373

ISBN 978-0-8048-4169-6

Distributed by

North America, Latin America & Europe
Tuttle Publishing
364 Innovation Drive
North Clarendon, VT 05759-9436 U.S.A.
Tel: 1 (802) 773-8930
Fax: 1 (802) 773-6993
info@tuttlepublishing.com
www.tuttlepublishing.com

Asia Pacific
Berkeley Books Pte. Ltd.
61 Tai Seng Avenue #02-12
Singapore 534167
Tel: (65) 6280-1330
Fax: (65) 6280-6290
inquiries@periplus.com.sg
www.periplus.com

Japan
Tuttle Publishing
Yaekari Building, 3rd Floor
5-4-12 Osaki, Shinagawa-ku
Tokyo 141 0032
Tel: (81) 3 5437-0171
Fax: (81) 3 5437-0755
sales@tuttle.co.jp
www.tuttle.co.jp

Indonesia
PT Java Books Indonesia
Jl. Rawa Gelam IV No. 9
Kawasan Industri Pulogadung
Jakarta 13930, Indonesia
Tel: 62 (21) 4682 1088
Fax: 62 (21) 461 0207
crm@periplus.co.id
www.periplus.co.id

First edition
15 14 13 12 11   10 9 8 7 6 5 4 3 2 1   1106TP

Printed in Singapore

CONTENTS

Foreword

Our role as gardeners is to choose, plant and tend the best seeds within the garden of our consciousness. Learning to look deeply at our consciousness is our greatest gift and our greatest need, for there lie the seeds of suffering and of love, the very roots of our being, of who we are. Mindfulness—itself a seed—is key to the care of this garden. It is the guide and the practice by which we learn how to use the seeds of suffering to nourish the seeds of love.

In *The Seeds of Love* Jerry Braza offers a translation of various wisdom traditions as insights on how to take care of the gardener—ourselves—and the garden—the soil of our consciousness. The mindfulness practices contained in this book are gardening tools that you will rely on again and again.

This is a book that will help anyone seeking to understand and nurture the seeds that create true love in self and others. Turn to these pages when you need a gentle reminder to tend the beautiful seeds of love that reside within.

—Thich Nhat Hanh
March 2011

Introduction

"Every blade of grass has its angel that bends over it and whispers, 'Grow, grow.'" —*The Talmud*

If ancient wisdom tells us that even a blade of grass needs encouragement, how much more do the people in our lives need us to whisper words of inspiration into their lives? Imagine the face of a child hearing, "You are so precious. You can do it. I'm so glad you were born." Picture the look on your loved one's face when you say, "You are perfect as you are. You are such a joy. I am here for you. Thank you for being in my life."

And if you received continual whispers of "You are enough, just as you are," how would your life be different? Would you be better able to whisper encouragement into the lives of those you love?

Gaining the wisdom and insights you need to grow and thrive in an atmosphere of love, compassion and kindness will prepare you to deeply water those seeds in the lives of others. As a partner, parent, family member or friend—we all want our relationships to grow in love. We long to love more deeply, remove barriers and open new pathways to love so we can find true happiness. It is within relationships, including our relationship with ourselves, that the seeds of love are born and nurtured—or not. Healthy, supportive relationships enrich our journey along life's path. They help define us and often teach us lessons we will need down the road. Are you ready to step out in faith? Our journey begins on a garden path.

Like a garden, relationships require thoughtful tending. With that image in mind, we will look deeply at the seeds that grow in the garden of our consciousness. We will discover how the practice of mindfulness, living in the present moment, can become our most valuable tool in nurturing the seeds of love and transforming the seeds of pain.

Growing up, I spent many hours helping my parents tend our backyard garden. The fruits of our labor offered nourishment during the long Wisconsin winters. But the effort of tending—tossing compost, tilling the soil, planting the seeds and watering the crops—offered rewards of its own, including the opportunity to witness the transformation of seeds coming to life. I'm sure my parents would be delighted today to find the garden has become both metaphor and muse to me, representing the fertile foundation of our spiritual and emotional well-being.

The seeds, both positive and negative, that are watered throughout our lives influence and affect the quality of our life from birth to death. Every interaction with people, situations, ideas—including what we consume and absorb from the media—impacts our senses and consciousness. Accessing the deep interior world of consciousness is like turning the soil of our garden. Whether we simply rake the surface or dig down to the roots, we are shaping the garden of our consciousness to develop a healthy self and positive relationships. If you are dedicated to tending your garden, you will become aware of seed consciousness and learn how to focus on nurturing healthy behaviors and transforming challenging life experiences.

In reflecting on our life as a garden, it is easy to see how we arrived where we are today based on the seeds that were watered within us. Parents and others, who nurture children in gentle, loving ways can bear witness to their efforts as they observe those children happily thriving and engaged in their growing lives. On the other hand, in my volunteer work with inmates at a local penitentiary, it is painfully clear that most of them had significant others in their lives who were far too generous in watering negatives seeds within their consciousness.

In most native traditions, grandparents teach children about life. "A fight is going on inside me," one Cherokee grandfather said to his grandson. "It is a terrible fight between two wolves. One is evil—he is anger, sorrow, regret, greed, resentment, inferiority, lies, superiority and ego. The other is good—he is joy, peace, love, hope, kindness, empathy, generosity and compassion. The same fight is going on inside you, and inside every other person, too."

The grandson pondered a moment and asked, "Which wolf will win?" The grandfather simply replied, "The one you feed."

The seeds of joy, compassion and loving-kindness are easily watered when we are truly present to others and celebrate their presence in our lives. Our crucial task is to visualize the people in our lives—even those who are just passing through—as a precious garden, to discover which seeds need watering and understand how exposure to negative elements can harm the budding sprouts if they are not tended properly.

To tend your spiritual and emotional garden, you'll need a working set of tools or skills to support and help you nurture the soil of your consciousness and the seeds that have been planted during your lifetime. Mindfulness, or the practice of being aware of the present moment, can become the greatest tool in your gardening efforts.

At some point in our lives, many of us become acutely aware of how mindlessly we have lived and how easy it is to be swept up in busyness and an incessant preoccupation with the future. While this realization usually comes with age, with wisdom it can be achieved at any time of life. Using the practice of mindfulness, we can look deeply at the seeds that will change or enhance the quality of our relationships. Mindfulness offers us an opportunity to step away from the distractions of life and learn to be here now to develop true presence and to understand that love and happiness are grounded in the present moment.

Gradually we learn that love is a verb as well as a noun, and that loving self and others requires action, practice and ongoing growth. Living in the present moment and watering the seeds of love within ourselves and others is the heart of what it means to live fully. Reflecting on the impermanence of life can create anxiety or the in-spiration and motivation to reach the end of our life's journey with a resounding "Yes!" to the question, "Did I love well?"

At the heart of this book are the teachings of one of the most beloved Zen Masters in world, Thich Nhat Hanh. This honored Vietnamese master has popularized the concept of mindfulness in the West, and he reminds us that one need not be a Buddhist to practice mindfulness. Through his beautiful writings on the seeds of consciousness, I became inspired to look deeply at the seeds that were watered in my own life and how they have affected my own relationships. When I received the honor of being ordained as a dharma teacher, Thich Nhat Hahn encouraged me to make "watering the seeds of love" the focus of my future work and the heart of my teaching. This concept soon became a powerful way for me to deepen and transform my relationships. I became aware of what qualities contribute to the development of love, and I grew through the challenge of transforming seeds that could be harm-ful to others and myself. I discovered how mindfulness is central to the development of love and paramount to discovering which seeds need watering.

My hope is that you will gain insights and inspiration that prompt you to become a master gardener, transforming the seeds that need healing and watering the seeds that need nurturing so you, too, may grow in love. Through the master gardener program, offered at many land-grant universities, students learn how to garden and then how to support others in their own gardening efforts.

Once you discover your ability to nurture certain qualities, you will blossom like the most beautiful garden before turning your influence to those you love.

Join me on this journey of becoming the master gardener of your life and your relationships. May it yield a bountiful harvest – one that will outlive you and become your legacy.

"Whether you tend a garden or not, you are the gardener of your own being, the seed of your destiny." —The Findhorn Community

PART 1

Nourishing the Gardener: Everyday Practices for Growing Mindful Relationships

"As is the gardener, such is the garden."   —*Hebrew Proverb*

The foundation for developing mindful and healthy relationships begins with ourselves. Three practices–Seeing, Renewing and Being–will support you as you become the master gardener of your life and your relationships.

In the first chapter, on Seeing, you will learn how to view each person with a "beginner's mind," how to be open and accepting, how to develop the qualities of faith and patience—all of which offer the foundation for a healthy relationship. The second chapter on Renewing offers you ways to renew yourself and your relationships through the Three S's—silence, space, stopping. The final chapter focuses on the practice of Being or mindfulness as a means of being present in an openhearted way to what is occurring in us and around us. It is a way of seeing, a lens that will help us water the seeds of love in ourselves and others.

CHAPTER 1

Seeing: It All Begins with the Gardener

"In the beginner's mind there are many possibilities, but in the expert's there are few." —*Shunryu Suzuki*

I take great pleasure in looking at my backyard garden through the year, and every time I do, I'm reminded of the many elements needed to promote its growth and vitality. Just the other day, my wife went to the nursery to choose a variety of annuals to place in more than fifteen pots on our patio. After patiently waiting several days for the rain to stop, she carefully arranged them by color and size, planting each with the right mix of fertilizer and compost soil. Pausing a moment to admire her artwork, she expressed her hopefulness and marveled at how the gardening process requires a certain attitude of openness and unconditional acceptance as to what will blossom.

Spring is the season of potential; new buds and tender shoots invite us to open ourselves to faith in possibilities. Summer is a season of growth and reward, as we see our labor come to fruition, pick the first tomato and zucchini and appreciate what several months of patience have brought. Fall, on the other hand, signifies harvest, a time for slowing down and preparing for a period of rest. Every season of the year offers us a mindset for contemplating the garden within our relationships and ourselves.

Just as the soil of the garden holds the seeds, bulbs and roots of the plants—including weeds—that we see above ground, so your heart holds the daily burdens, the stresses of life and the challenges that face us all—especially those that awaken us in the middle of the night. Use the garden metaphor as a starting point from which to expand and explore new ways of seeing yourself and your life. What would it be like to be open to life in a new way? To start accepting yourself rather than judging? To truly believe in yourself, so that you can thrive with faith and patience? Sometimes it takes us a while to realize certain behaviors or mindsets aren't working and that we can't solve yesterday's problems with old ideas or actions. Start to see yourself with new possibilities and hear the whisper, "grow, grow."

Beginner's Mind (Openness)

As a university professor, I was expected to be an expert, and yet intuitively I always knew that having the mind of a beginner or of someone who has retained the natural curiosity of a child would be a greater asset to learning. I find truth in Suzuki's belief that "In the beginner's mind there are many possibilities, but in the expert's there are few." Learning to see others and life from a child's perspective, with an open mind and heart, is the mindset of a beginner.

One of my former students was paraplegic and had visible deformities. He was a delight to have in class. He made his way around campus on a gurney-style cart, lying prone and navigating by moving a small ball with his mouth. I recall him sharing his story about how children would often approach him with questions and comments: "What happened to your legs?" or "Cool cart!" While the children, with their beginners' minds, were openly curious and naturally accepting, their parents, on the other hand, were often embarrassed, fearful or judgmental.

How can we, as adults, regain that beginner's mind? We must begin by letting go of the baggage of past experience and perception-shaping memories. Without them, our minds are clear to accept ourselves and others, allowing us to see in a fresh new way. Living as a beginner offers the ideal mindset for learning, teaching and relationships. Think how refreshing it would be to encounter a familiar person but be consciously able to see them as if for the first time, with no preconceived notions of who they are, no baggage, no memories to shape your perception. "Habit energies"—our mindless or robotic way of seeing things—often cloud the way we see others, especially those who are closest to us. Contrast our perceptions with those of children, who are captivated each moment with delight and discovery. This comparison offers a reminder and paradox for us on how we can experience others and ourselves without the models we've built of how we "should" be and do.

Unconditional Acceptance and Non-Judgmental Mind

Imagine how it feels to know that you have people in your life who love you and accept you unconditionally, without judgment. These people see you perfectly, just as you are, and you don't have to work to prove yourself or gain their acceptance. What would that feel like for you? Now stop to consider how you think about others. How often do you find yourself trying to change someone? How much energy do you invest in trying to "fix" things about them or change their behaviors or decisions? Because most of us have learned to be judgmental of ourselves, it's only natural that we judge—and even reject—others.

When we love someone, we want what is best for them, yet our desire to help is often clouded by our own perception of what is best. That perception may be based on what we want rather than on what they need. In gardens, as in life, growth can only take place when we accept conditions as they are. One of my favorite mantras, "It is what it is," can be very helpful in creating a foundation of acceptance from which we can learn ways to nurture the qualities that sustain life and transform the qualities that detract from it.

Unconditional acceptance of others springs from a deep, unconditional acceptance of ourselves. How often do we focus our attention on minor outward imperfections and not on our true character? Unfortunately we often have only a superficial awareness of what is going on in others and ourselves, and our focus is far too often on negative rather than positive attributes.

> *"Imagine that half the world is hidden from you. Half of the person sitting across from you has never been appreciated, half of the garden has never been seen or smelled, half of your own life has never been truly witnessed and appraised."* —Arthur Zajonc

If we truly love someone, we must begin from the position of unconditional acceptance, both of the half we see and the half we don't. We must embrace those unseen facets as the mystery and the journey of discovering our partner in relationship. Loving others requires acceptance and a nonjudgmental attitude, despite what we see as their vulnerabilities and imperfections. It means loving the other not only when they are pleasing us or making us happy, so that our actions say, "I love you because of who you are and not only what supports my ego." When we hold an underlying judgment or a need for someone to be different, that is what shapes our view of our loved one. In such cases, our words or behaviors may say, "I love you if you conform to my needs and expectations." It is easy to perceive others in this way when the seed of judgment within us has been watered and reinforced. Over time judgment can grow into resentment, and once resentment springs up, it is impossible to truly love.

Think of a time when you met someone, and your initial impression caused you to form a certain judgment about them. Future encounters may continue to build on this early judgment to the point of becoming a stereotype. Without being mindful of the judgment you have made, you may spend months and even years allowing your belief to overshadow that person's true self, capabilities, and personality.

I admit I have done this myself, unconsciously creating a perception of students on the first day of class on the basis of their personalities or perceived capabilities. One such person entered my class, and it was easy to see he had experienced some kind of accident or trauma that led to a disability. At first I was not sure how best to support him to facilitate his learning. I knew I needed to create an understanding, so I invited him to visit during my office hours. In only a short time, he shared how two near-fatal accidents had left him with permanent disabilities. Beneath a façade of physical struggle was a strong person who overcame many odds to survive and succeed. By quickly moving beyond the stereotype and viewing him with unconditional love and acceptance, I discovered this person's true potential–and, more important, he discovered his own worth and potential. The acceptance he found allowed him to excel far beyond anyone's expectations, including his own. He took all of my classes and eventually became a teaching assistant. After five years and nearly weekly meetings, he graduated with a master's degree. He grew in love and constantly demonstrated gratitude for all those who supported him. At graduation, in addition to giving me a copy of his master's project, he presented me with a book he wrote called "Wednesdays with Jerry." Imagine what a different outcome could have occurred if I had judged him during our first encounter.

Faith

We create the greatest potential for growth by first selecting the best seeds. In choosing seeds, we demonstrate faith that they will sprout into healthy growth, and we need faith as we wait for that growth before we can enjoy the flowers and fruits.

> *"We are the gardeners who identify, water, and cultivate the best seeds. We need some faith that there are good seeds within us, and then, with appropriate attention, we need to touch those seeds while we go through our day."* —Thich Nhat Hanh

Just as we instinctively know a seed will sprout, our faith in others is instinctual as well. It is an underlying philosophy that supports our very being. A child has faith that his mother is there to meet his needs, or she believes her favorite blanket will comfort and protect her. We all desire a safe and solid place to stand—a refuge where we are accepted—and we have faith that such a place exists. The haven of relationship is where we first learn faith, where we test our wings and learn the skills we need from each other so each of us can grow.

When my wife and I chose our wedding rings, we decided jointly to have a green stone as the focal point of each ring to remind us of our growth together. That choice more thirty years ago has become the focus of our relationship—to have unconditional love for and faith in each other, to grow as individuals and to commit to the continuing growth of our relationship. Regardless of the type of relationship, growth relies on faith, and in turn causes faith to increase.

> *"Those who do not have faith in others will not be able to stand on their own. Those who are always suspicious will be lonely."*
> —*Sheng Yen, (from Jack Kornfield's* The Buddha is Still Teaching: Contemporary Buddhist Wisdom*)*

Patience

In an era of instant communication and fast food, our reliance on modern conveniences makes it all too easy for us to expect instant gratification and immediate results. Unfortunately, that expectation spills over into other areas of our lives, including gardening. I recall my curiosity regarding the slow growth of my spinach plants. Wondering why they were taking so much time to bloom, I started to pull out a few tiny sprouts. Almost immediately I noticed how, in my impatience, I destroyed the roots and the potential for growth. In relationships as in the garden, growth takes time. Expecting others to bloom before they are ready is like trying to force spinach to grow faster.

In moving through your day, seek a mindset of openness to see each person and experience each moment with the eyes of a child. See your spouse, family and friends as if for the first time. Letting go of what happened in the past, open your eyes and heart. With unconditional acceptance, faith and patience, see how they go through seasons of growth and blooming.

> *"Real patience requires a gentle willingness to let life unfold at its own pace. This willingness, in turn, requires mindfulness."*
> —Joan Borysenko

Practice:
- Reflect on what it felt like when you have received unconditional love, acceptance and faith. How did this help you to see yourself and others differently?
- How would your life be different if you started to see and experience life as a child—as if doing, seeing and feeling everything for the first time?
- What would your life be like if you discovered something new about yourself every day? Move beyond the part that is visible to explore the mystery containing your wholeness—the parts that are often hidden and buried within.

CHAPTER 2

Renewing: Taking Care
of the Gardener

"If I'm not for myself, who will be for me? If I am only for myself what am I? If not now, when?" —*Rabbi Hillel*

Do you ever take time to pause, be quiet and find space in your busy life? Too often we fill our lives with busyness because we're afraid of what may arise during times of silence, space and quiet. What are we trying to avoid?

Experienced farmers know the value of resting the land or allowing the soil to "go fallow." They rotate crops from one section of the field to the next, and every several years they stop planting in certain sections for a season or two to rest the land and revitalize the soil. In the Bible, people are instructed not to plow the land every seventh year, allowing the poor to take from it what grows so that both the land and disadvantaged benefit. This was in keeping with the custom of the Sabbath or the seventh day as a day of rest. Like the land and our gardens, the gardener too needs time to rest and renew.

Contrary to taking time for renewal, our society is caught in an epidemic of "hurry sickness." Everyone keeps so busy and, as William James said, "They live in a state of ceaseless frenzy, thinking they should be doing something more than they are doing in the moment."

Recently I spent time visiting the Washington, D.C. area. My daily routine was to drive to the train station, arriving early enough to find a parking space before embarking on Amtrak. After the forty-minute ride, the glut of passengers maneuvered to disembark and exit the station, walking quickly to their offices. Once, on my commute home, I dropped my Metro card at the turnstile, and with that seconds-long mistake, I missed the next train. This started a cascading series of events that required me to run six blocks down a busy urban street in time for an appointment. Despite my practice of mindfulness, I found I was easily immersed in the milieu and energy of this fast-paced environment in which so many seemed at ease, After several days I remembered when that frenzied lifestyle— minus the train—was once my everyday pattern.

While this type of hurry sickness is rare for me now, I am attuned to those seeds in me and easily become aware of people around me living in this frenzied way day after day, seldom having—or taking—time to stop, calm themselves, and take refuge. Every living thing seeks the security and refuge of a resting place, be that place in nature or in some quiet structure. Where might you find that refuge in your life?

"Refuge," however, can be misleading. False refuge is hiding through busyness, fear, alcohol, drugs and food—anything to numb the pain of what is happening and avoid looking deeply at the challenges we may be experiencing. True refuge enjoyed in the present moment by purposely returning to ourselves to reconnect with who we are and what we are experiencing. When we are able to take refuge in loving self and others, then we have arrived in a place of security and love. Refuge in nature and self includes opportunities for the Three S's: *silence*, finding *space* in our busy lives, and taking time to *stop* and rest along the way.

Silence

I regularly find true refuge at a local monastery, where the public is invited to come for prayer, reflection and meditation. As time permits, I spend the day reflecting, resting and writing. On one of these recent sojourns, I was struck by the silence and absence of outside stimuli except for the rare sound of a distant car. It was wonderful walking through the wild flowers and neatly planted gardens surrounding the modest buildings. Often after a day in this environment, I come away renewed. Retreating from the outside world provides solace and rest for mind, body and spirit. At the monastery there is a pamphlet for visitors, an invitation to enter "quietude," to take stock of our lives and open ourselves to be available to a higher wisdom. A sign outside of the meditation hall reads, "Silence is as deep as eternity." This environment fosters an opportunity to listen deeply.

In silence the mind naturally quiets, allowing both mind and body to mirror the outside environment. It is easier to slow our thinking and take time to focus on our habitual patterns—such as worry and fear—and redirect our minds to wholesome and renewing thoughts. Even a short time in a quiet environment can be enough to offer rest and renewal. No elaborate method or preparation is needed to benefit from silence, only the aspiration to make silence a priority.

Through my meditation practice I have learned that, even in this slowing of the mind, thoughts are present, though our minds are not as "reactive" to them in solitude and the natural environment. We can learn to observe our worries and fears just as we observe the flowers and wildlife that surround us in this natural refuge—possibly in our own backyard. You may not have the luxury of a trip to the monastery to take refuge from your busy life; however, a slow walk, a visit to a park, or sitting on the porch or patio may offer the same healing benefits.

The absence of outside noise makes it easier to form a deeper connection to nature and others. Perhaps the single quality that defines all mystical traditions is "Interbeing," often described as oneness with all. After spending time in nature or attending retreats, I often leave feeling renewed and connected to nature and others in deeper ways. By entering the stream of silence, I experience Interbeing in personal ways. While I am often alone in these silent places, I feel a connection with everything, and I am never lonely.

In various traditions of meditation there is the concept of "noble silence," which means unifying body, speech and mind as we go through the day. In noble silence, you are encouraged not to talk except for essential communication required with meals or chores. In silence it is easier to quiet the mind because there is no need to constantly respond to multiple conversations and dialogue. We have enough self-talk occurring constantly in our own minds. The more I practice noble silence, the more I am slowly finding as much joy in between words and in the presence of others without a need for a constant verbal expression of every thought.

"Silence is something that comes from our own hearts, and not from someone outside. If we are truly silent, then no matter what situation we find ourselves in, we can enjoy the silence. Silence does not only mean not talking and not doing loud things. Silence means that we're not disturbed inside, there's no talking inside."
—*Thich Nhat Hanh*

Space

Every summer we are amazed at how certain perennials take over certain spaces in the garden. Year after year we have to thin the crocosmia to create room for less-hardy plants to find space and light.

In our busy lives, creating space for the activities of "being" vs. "doing" always brings renewal and healing. I used to find it easy to fill my daily schedule to the brim, like a cup of coffee with little room for cream. The other day when I stopped for my favorite brew, the barista asked, "Do you want it with room?"—meaning did I want room to add cream. Every time I hear that phrase, I am reminded that it's okay to have fewer appointments, lunches or coffee dates and leave room for quiet time and reflection. The awareness that "less is often more" may become more important with age, or perhaps with wisdom.

When asked why his music was so beautiful, a famous pianist responded, "I strike the keys like most other musicians. It is the space between the notes that makes it beautiful." The space between notes and the space between objects is what offers contrast and beauty. One of my favorite hobbies is photography, and one of my favorite subjects, as you can probably guess, is flowers. Finding space and distinction between the flowers offers contrast and beauty, and enough light for seeing these things.

> *"What makes a fire burn is space between the logs. A breathing space. Too much of a good thing, too many logs packed too tightly, can douse the flames just like a pail of water would. So building fires requires attention to the spaces in between as much as to the wood…. A fire grows simply because the space is there in which the flame that knows how to burn will find its way."* —Judy Brown

Stopping and Resting

Just as gardens need time to renew during the winter, and plots of farmland need to rest for a year or more to yield better crops in the future, we need to take time to stop and rest. Inherent in all religious traditions is a time for rest and renewal. Whether it be Shabbat or Sabbath, or just "lazy day," the results of self-renewal are the same.

Growing up, Sunday was a day of rest for my family, one that began with church, followed by a special breakfast and relaxation time. Later in the afternoon we would enjoy the best meal of the week. Other nearby family members often joined us for these meals, which were typically enjoyed in a local park or by a lake in the summertime. After eating together, my cousins and I would either swim or play in the park. We celebrated the Sabbath without any major effort, and we always felt renewed. The day became more challenging as it wore on, since Monday meant back to school. Yet I always felt better knowing that at least for one day, we felt rested and renewed.

31

"In our consciousness there are wounds also, lots of pains. Our consciousness also needs to rest in order to restore itself. Our consciousness is just like our body. Our body knows how to heal itself if we allow it the chance to do so. The same thing is true with our consciousness; our consciousness knows how to heal itself if we know how to allow it to do so. But we don't allow it. We always try to do something. We worry so much about healing, which is why we do not get the healing we need. Only if we know how to allow them to rest can our body and our soul heal themselves."

—*Thich Nhat Hanh*

Wanting bountiful growth each spring, we let our garden beds go barren during the winter months. So too we need to prune our lives of too much doing, and lie fallow at times so that we can listen to our bodies, thoughts and feelings. Through silence we listen to what is needed, through space we see the beauty that is in and around us, and by stopping we are truly able to enjoy life and those we love.

Practice:
- In what ways do you find time to stop in your daily and weekly routines?
- Reflect on someone or something that represents beauty in your life. How does the condition of space play a role in enhancing this beauty?
- During the silent moments of your life, what is it that emerges— moments of delight or moments of fear?

Regardless of your schedule, find times to be silent, create space and stop along the way.

"Between stimulus and response there is a space. In that space is our power to choose our response. In our response lies our growth and our freedom." —*Viktor E. Frankl*

CHAPTER 3

Being: Watering the Seed of Mindfulness

"Of all the meditative wisdom practices that have developed in traditional cultures throughout the world and throughout history, mindfulness is perhaps the most basic, the most powerful, the most universal, among the easiest to grasp and engage in, and arguably, the most sorely needed now. For mindfulness is none other than the capacity we all already have to know what is actually happening as it is happening." —Jon Kabat Zinn

At a recent meditation retreat, I spoke with a woman who had been a doctor before joining the monastic community as a teacher. I asked her, "Do you still practice medicine?" After a long pause, she looked directly into my eyes and said, "Brother, mindfulness is the best medicine." I have shared this story with others, including a friend who has experienced stage-four cancer, who said, "Mindfulness practice has saved my life." Whether we are ill or healthy, we should always focus on improving the quality of our lives.

In learning to care for ourselves as gardeners, we sought to have a beginner's mind, including openness, faith, patience and acceptance so as to see in new ways. We also learned that we require silence, space and stopping to rest so we can renew ourselves. Mindfulness is a practice that supports everything else we have learned thus far. It means learning to be present in an openhearted way to what is occurring in us and around us. Mindfulness is the practice of bringing our whole being to everything we do. It is a way of seeing—a lens—that will help us cultivate the seeds of love in others and ourselves. Mindfulness itself is a seed that, when watered, strengthens and grows, making us more alive and vibrant in the process, like a rose bush receiving the right nutrients, sunlight and water.

How wonderful it is to walk out into a beautiful garden, which offers a vision of what might be cultivated in the gardens of our homes and our consciousness through mindfulness. The practice of mindfulness is the ability to be truly aware and see what is happening within outer gardens and the gardens of our consciousness. The key practice and the essence of becoming a "master gardener" of our consciousness is to know how to nourish the seed of mindfulness.

"The practice is to nourish the seed of mindfulness so that it becomes a positive 'habit energy' and a means of transforming suffering in the form of negative seeds." — *Thich Nhat Hanh*

Mindful or Mindless?

Scattered weeds in the garden are no different than the stress we experience in our lives. Spiritual teacher and author of *The Power of Now*, Eckart Tolle says, "Stress is caused by being 'here' but wanting to be 'there,' or being in the present but wanting to be in the future. It's a split that tears you apart inside." If we learned to focus on each moment and live fully in the present, we wouldn't be swayed by the angst of the past or the worries or dreams of the future. As Matthew 6:34 reminds us, "Do not worry about tomorrow, for tomorrow will worry about itself."

Just as we have formed the habit energies of being in the past or the future, we have also unconsciously trained ourselves not to be in the here and now. In the same way we have learned to be "mindless," we can consciously cultivate the positive habit energy of being mindful through an ongoing awareness of where our attention is at any given moment. We could be in Monet's garden in

Giverny but miss its beauty if we're preoccupied by some concern. We could be sitting with our beloved, but if our mind is elsewhere, we are missing out on giving and receiving love, and on life itself, which is ultimately found only in the present moment.

> *"Nothing ever happened in the past that can prevent you from being present now; and if the past cannot prevent you from being present now, what power does it have?"* —Eckhart Tolle

When we are mindful, there is an awareness of what is happening in the present moment. We are fully experiencing our thoughts, feelings and what is happening within our bodies. We are conscious of our actions, whether it be walking to our car, eating a meal, or taking a drive in the country. We are more likely to move slowly through the day, attentive to what is happening and enjoying every moment, even daily rituals, as if they were happening for the first time.

When we are mindless, there is the tendency to operate on automatic pilot. We struggle to stay on task, and we frequently multitask without realizing what we are doing. We find ourselves hurrying to reach our goal, only to find it difficult to slow down enough to enjoy reaching it.

Of course these are extremes, and most of the time operate with qualities of both mindfulness and mindlessness. In our aspiration to be more mindful, remember it is best to keep a "beginner's mind" and an acceptance of what is happening in the present moment.

Mindfulness Is Being Aware and Remembering

When a famous teacher was asked what practice is most important, he always responded with one word—"Awareness!" Thinking he would expound on such a brief answer, students would often ask again, and again his response was "Awareness!" Our first step in cultivating the seed of mindfulness is to become aware of what we are experiencing within our body, mind and feelings at any given moment. This practice seems obvious, but think about the last time you talked with a friend. Were you truly with them, or was your mind focused on what your next response might be, or on other thoughts and feelings?

Coupled with awareness is the ability to remember. On a stained glass window at the Deer Park monastery in Escondido, California, there are three Sanskrit words: Smirti, Samadhi and Prajna. Smiriti is the word for mindfulness and translated literally means "to remember." Samadhi is translated to mean "concentration," and Prajna refers to "wisdom" or "insight." So with awareness we are able to focus, gain insight, and discover if we are truly present to what is happening. With awareness we are more likely to remember what is important about a given moment, and every time we return to the present moment we cultivate the seed of mindfulness.

Make it a practice to remember to return fully to whatever you are engaged in at the present moment. This is not about remembering the past or to pick up a loaf of bread on the way home—it is to remember to return to this moment. Are you living it fully or off in a trance? If we allow ourselves to be easily swayed by every thought that arises, we will face far greater challenges in deeply enjoying the people and experiences in our life. By simply remembering to return to what you are doing now, you already have begun to water the seed of mindfulness.

"The heart of most spiritual practices is simply this: Remember who you are. Remember what you love. Remember what is sacred. Remember what is true. Remember that you will die and that this day is a gift. Remember how you wish to live." —Wayne Muller

Cultivating Mindfulness

As we have learned, mindfulness is a process of being in the present moment, and it is cultivated by being aware, remembering, and returning again and again to what is happening. It is a practice of controlling our wandering minds. The acronym WIN—What's

Important Now—can remind us of this practice. This phrase can become a wonderful mantra for prioritizing your focus despite the many demands competing for your attention at any given time.

The ideal way to develop mindfulness is through the practice of meditation. When we meditate, we simply attend to what is happening in that moment. If we are formally meditating, our attention is often focused on our breath or a word or phrase. If we are tending to the garden, our focus is on the planting, weeding and watering. Whether in formal meditation or informally connecting with daily life, we can apply the insights from meditation and other contemplative practices, such as prayer, to everyday life. In many small ways, we can learn ways to stop and calm ourselves in every moment. Once we have gained this realization we are able to look deeply and create understanding of what is happening NOW. With the ability to stop, calm and look deeply we slowly discover that we are practicing and watering the seed of mindfulness.

Stopping

The first step in any type of meditation—and the key to developing mindfulness—is learning how to stop. In stopping, we let go of the past and future and dwell in the present moment. Each day offers us many opportunities to cultivate the art of stopping—stop signs, people, bells, or an entire day of rest such as the Sabbath. Stopping does not require us to come to a halt; rather, we are to pause and heed what is happening in the moment.

What might stopping look like in your life? Take a moment to lay this book aside, stop reading—in fact, stop everything for the next several minutes, and just *be*. Now, explore what you've just experienced. Typically, people discover sights they haven't been seeing, sounds they haven't been hearing. They become aware of the busyness and over-activity of the their minds.

Learning to stop requires a conscious awareness and a cultivation of this skill. Two practices that support stopping—bells and gratitude—require us to bring our attention fully into the present moment, which often works best by taking a conscious breath or two to center yourself in the moment.

Bells

Historically temple and church bells have reminded people to stop and pray, reflect or meditate. They announce the time of day, alert us to special events, and remind us who may need our support. Whether the ringing of a phone or the oven timer at the end of its cycle, "bells of mindfulness" are a reminder to stop, to pause.

In meditation, bells are a metaphor for mindful awareness, but other reminders can be just as effective. Several years ago, a deaf student took my mindfulness course. Aware that she could not hear the bell, I asked her what "bells of mindfulness" she could incorporate into her life. She responded very tenderly with the help of her signer, "My baby is my bell of mindfulness. Every time I hold her and feed her, I feel fully present, and at no other time do I feel so mindful. I recognize that I naturally breathe more slowly, and in the process we both become more relaxed and connected. These are moments of great joy and peace."

One of my joys is the opportunity to perform wedding ceremonies. During the service, I use a large bell to invite guests to pause and reflect on various important parts of the ceremony. In my parting words to the couple, I recommend that they stop when they hear bells and remember their commitment to each other. The bells of our lives offer reminders of the preciousness of life, the sacredness of the moment, and the value of each other.

Ideally your practice will reach the point where no sound is necessary, and just the thought or sight of your loved one is enough to cause you to pause and be mindful of your relationships. At those times, stop and take a breath, enjoy the present moment, and heed the call to mindfulness.

"Temple bells stop but the sound keeps coming out in the flowers"
—*Basho*

Gratitude

Every day presents countless opportunities to stop and appreciate the moment. When such a moment arises, reflect on all the people and gifts that have made that moment possible, and be grateful for them. Gratefulness keeps us in the present moment. Theologian Meister Eckhart said, "If the only prayer we ever said was 'Thank you,' it would suffice." My favorite simple practice is to stop and be present with everyone who offers a service, such as the clerk at the post office, the barista at the coffee shop, or the gas station attendant. I offer a genuine smile and say, "Thank you for being here and for your wonderful service."

Calming

Another function of meditation and a key to developing mindfulness is focusing, which is best developed by calming ourselves. I tend to find it easier to stop and much more challenging to calm and quiet my busy mind. One of the most powerful things we can do to strengthen the "muscle" of our attention and mindfulness is to return to what we are doing over and over again throughout the day. Try not to get frustrated, and remember the words of St. Francis de Sales, "Even if you bring yourself back 1,000 times, it will be worth it." Calming strengthens our concentration by focusing on something repetitively, such as our breath, mantras or short phrases, prayers and flowers. Calming will also help us recognize and become aware of feelings and bodily sensations when they arise. As we become quiet we then have the opportunity to embrace these feelings.

When we are calm we learn to recognize what is happening in the present moment. In this state we can deeply experience this moment through our sense and feelings and learn to accept this moment as it is. The recognition of one breath is often enough to bring us back, help us focus, and strengthen our ability to concentrate.

You practiced stopping earlier. This time, stop and place your attention on something. Focus on the senses—truly note what you are seeing and hearing. Focus on your breath—experience fully the in-breath and out-breath, and continue doing this for a few minutes. Notice that as you focus on something, just for a moment, other thoughts and worries naturally recede and the mind becomes calmer. Whatever your point of our focus, be it our senses or the person we are with, focusing can help us to calm ourselves.

Looking Deeply

In stopping and calming, we have learned to become more relaxed and mindful in the present moment. At this point we have the concentration needed to look deeply, and discover and understand the source of our current feelings. This process will be invaluable as we explore the various seeds in the garden of our consciousness. "Hello, Anger. Where did you come from? Why are you here at this time?"

In looking deeply we will also discover in the ones we love the reasons they are suffering, and we will be able to clearly see that their suffering is also our suffering. By using mindfulness, you will discover ways to look deeply at the seeds that need tending within yourself and others.

Practices to Develop Mindfulness

We need a variety of practices to deepen this skill and strengthen the habit energy of mindfulness, just as we need a variety of exercises to strengthen our bodies. These practices can be easily integrated into our daily life, affording us moments to remember, stop, calm, and return to the present moment.

MINDFUL BREATHING

Breathing in, I calm my body; breathing out, I smile.

Our life begins with breath and ends with breath. The average individual takes nearly 20,000 breaths each day. By stopping to practice conscious breathing at different times during the day, we are able to calm ourselves with the awareness of our in-breath and out-breath, inhalation and exhalation. In this practice, mind and body are connected, and the word "respiration" takes on its root meaning—to "re-spirit." By dwelling in each moment with breath as our anchor, we cultivate the energy and seed of mindfulness. When practicing mindful breathing, thoughts subside, the energy of mindfulness is encouraged, and we return instantly to fully experiencing the present moment.

MINDFUL WALKING

The practice of mindful walking is simply that of learning to be aware of each step you take. We often walk with little awareness, our mind focused on getting somewhere and often getting there quickly. The challenge in mindful walking is to walk knowing that you are walking. You bring your walking into your awareness so that walking itself becomes a form of meditation. Each step brings us back to our breath and the present moment. It is the bridge between the formal practice of meditation and informal activity of everyday life. When we walk only briefly in this way, we are reminded that our life is a walk. The more we become aware of our steps, the more we find peace along the way.

ANSWERING THE PHONE

Our technology-laden world offers countless possibilities to cultivate mindfulness. Cell phones, office phones and other bells can become invitations to stop, breathe, smile, and calm before engaging in dialogue. For example, when the phone rings, you could say a mantra before answering, such as, "Breathing in, I calm my body;

breathing out, I relax." My wife and I have a practice of stopping to breathe every time our Westminster-style chime strikes on the hour. Our answering machine message greets callers with, "Breathe and smile! You have reached the Brazas." These and other simple, daily, focused actions enhance the energy of mindfulness.

MINDFUL EATING

This simple practice focuses on the total enjoyment of your meal. Taking time to eat quietly for ten minutes before talking can offer a refuge of peace and time to appreciate the food. Slowing down long enough to recognize how many hands brought this food to our plates helps us to be truly grateful for this meal. With this sense of gratitude, the entire meal is the blessing. In every bite we have the opportunity to cultivate mindfulness by recognizing the amount, taste, and nourishment this food is providing our bodies. Being mindful of each bite and eating more slowly can also be an effective weight-loss plan and an antidote to careless eating.

> *"Engaging in mindful eating, even if only for a few minutes, can help you recognize how the practice of mindfulness encompasses all spheres and activities, including ordinary tasks."*
> —*Thich Nhat Hanh*

UNI-TASK VS. MULTI-TASK

The stress of life is often the result of doing more than one thing at a time. In our world, multi-tasking has become the norm, and most people take pride in their ability to do several things at once. This preoccupation with speed and doing more is the antithesis of mindfulness. Cultivating our garden helps us remember that multi-tasking is not effective. It is best to plant, weed and water the garden, one task at a time. In gardening and in life, learning to focus on one task at a time helps us perform each task more thoroughly and enjoy each more fully.

Many participants at my retreats and seminars are quick to remind me of their many responsibilities and insist that they will never complete their work unless they multi-task. My response is to gently remind them that every moment is an opportunity to learn behaviors that both improve our performance and enhance the quality of our lives. Mindfulness reminds us to see value in quality, rather than simply in performance.

Moments Make Up the Fabric of Our Lives.

A pioneer in studies on death and dying, the late Dr. Elisabeth Kübler-Ross said, "At the end of one's life, we don't remember how much money we had or our beautiful homes, we remember moments with loved ones." Most likely we recall a few moments from every day despite the thousands of moments we experience in our final days and months. Daniel Kahneman, Nobel Prize–winning scientist, suggests that we experience 20,000 moments each day, defined as a few seconds during which our brain records an experience. Thus the quality of our days is determined by how our brains recognize and categorize our moments—positive, negative or neutral—and the determiner is mindfulness. Were you there for those moments?

Why Be Mindful

Mindfulness offers a means of capturing those moments that make up the fabric of our lives. Since writing *Moment by Moment: The Art and Practice of Mindfulness*, I find the concept of mindfulness has become more than a word or an idea. For me it has become a philosophy that has transformed the quality of my life. I now see that most of what I considered stress in my life has typically been caused by past and future thinking. Through mindfulness, joy is more available—moment by moment—in the smile of a child, in a sunset, and in delight over a new flower in the garden. In writing and working, my productivity is increased by an ability to stay focused and concentrated on the task at hand. Most important, my personal and professional relationships have been deepened through an ability to truly be there for others.

> *"The practice of mindfulness requires only that whatever you do you do with your whole being."* —*Thich Nhat Hanh*

Practice:
- What keeps you from living in the present moment?
- Are you waiting to be happy? I'll be happy when…If only…What keeps you from being happy now? Reflect on your life as a movie. During what moments did you feel most alive?
- How can you create happiness in the "here and now"?

PART 2

The Soil:
Exploring Our Consciousness

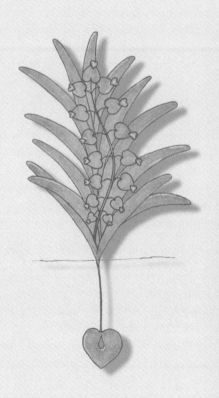

Don't go outside your house to see the flowers.
My friend, don't bother with that excursion.
Inside your body there are flowers.
One flower has a thousand petals.
That will do for a place to sit.
Sitting there you will have a glimpse of beauty
inside the body and out of it,
before gardens and after gardens.

—*Kabir*

After caring for and preparing your self through mindfulness, you—
the gardener—are ready to explore the soil of your consciousness.
This journey will lead you to develop a relationship with the present
moment and the garden of your consciousness. You will till the soil
of the mind and store consciousness—what you are aware of above
the soil and what often lies dormant below the soil in the storehouse
of your consciousness. You will learn to nurture and weed by watering the seeds of love (the wholesome seeds) and transforming the
seeds of suffering (the negative seeds). And if you aren't already
familiar with mantra practice, you will discover a new means of
actively nourishing the qualities needed to become a true master
gardener. See if you find truth in the concept that what you focus
on is what you become.

CHAPTER 4

Pathways to the Present Moment

"Don't turn away, keep your eyes on the wounded place—that is where the light enters." —*Rumi*

By developing the habit energies of seeing, renewing and being, we created the foundation for nourishing ourselves as gardeners and living fully in the present moment. Now we are prepared to apply mindfulness as a means of looking deeply to at the soil of our consciousness, allowing us to explore, experience and become intimate with every aspect of our being in each moment. Our practice of stopping and calming cultivates the habit energy of mindfulness, in which we can use **WIN** (**W**hat's **I**mportant **N**ow) to help us focus on the present moment. This morning I spent nearly twenty minutes walking mindfully with our dog, Bailey, slowly meandering a wooded park trail. Bailey reminded me to enjoy the journey as he mindfully attended to every tree, every bird, and every squirrel.

"Be in awe of all that is alive. Be in natural wonder. It is the piece of peace." —*Gunilla Norris*

Once we are actively aware and concentrating, we can begin to reflect on the various aspects or pathways that make up the present moment. By looking deeply, we explore the meaning of what is happening and learn to develop true intimacy with others and ourselves. We must be aware, be observant, and be open to understanding what we observe.

In Buddhism, the pathways to understanding the present moment are called the five aggregates—a collection of characteristics that make up the present. These five aspects include our body, feelings, perceptions, mental formations (the stories we create) and our consciousness. These qualities define the present moment and provide a foundation for understanding how a seed may start as a sprout and develop through positive and negative memories. In stopping, calming and looking deeply, we can understand the relationship between mind, body and consciousness.

Work of the Master Gardener

Reflect back on the moments of your life that seem most significant—moments when you were acutely aware of your body, your feelings, your perceptions, your stories. A famous Korean Zen Master said there is only one important question to ask, over and over again: "What is this?" By working to discover and experience what is happening in the present moment, we will find the basis of true intimacy, happiness and making deep connections with others and ourselves.

Master gardeners must hone their abilities to turn the soil and unearth an understanding of their very being. I remember as a child playing for hours with a shovel in a pile of dirt—exploring, building and trying to understand what is below the surface. As George Bernard Shaw once said, "The best place to see God is in a garden. You can dig for her." This work requires a process of exploring, in the present moment, the various components making up the fabric of our life.

Through mindfulness, we can ford the flowing rivers opening from the mouth of each moment. These tributaries are the five aggregates—body, feelings, perceptions, mental formations/stories and consciousness.

Body

Recently I had the unnerving experience of waking up with a back spasm so severe that it took enormous energy to even attempt to get out of bed. In that moment, I was highly attuned to the messages of my body—severely constricted back muscles, painful tension in my entire body, constricted breathing and subsequent fear and panic.

It was easier for me to minimize the impact of this pain by breathing and becoming aware of what was happening. Quickly I understood that my body initiated a stress response exacerbated by my pain and irrational thinking. By stopping and calming myself in that moment, the wrenching pain gradually subsided and I could eventually get up and get help.

The best doorway to the present moment and barometer to gauge our well-being is to check in with our body. What are you seeing, hearing, tasting, smelling and touching? How are your breathing—from your chest? diaphragm? Is it labored?; What is your heart rate and muscle tension telling you about what's happening now? Learning mindfulness begins with learning to check in with our bodies.

"No way we can avoid what's in our body. The truth about our childhood is stored up in our body. Although we can repress it, we can never alter it, our intellect, and our body tripped with medication. But some day it will present its bill." —Alice Miller

Feelings

We record memories of our lives in terms of positive and negative experiences that influence our overall mood and offer depth to each moment. When we recall significant experiences in our lives, we can rediscover moments in which our current thoughts and feelings were first activated. In working with groups I often ask, "When did you feel most alive? Describe that moment." People often share tender or powerful moments such as the birth of a child, experiencing a brilliant sunset or the antics of a playful puppy.

Feelings are typically pleasant, unpleasant or neutral. Every day these feelings wake us up or lull us into a state of complacency. Learning to be with each of these feelings is the essence of mindfulness. As the poet Rumi says in "The Guest House":

> *This being human is a guesthouse.*
> *Every morning is a new arrival.*
> *A joy, a depression, meanness,*
> *Some momentary awareness comes*
> *As an unexpected visitor.*
> *Welcome and entertain them all!*

The key is to become aware of various feelings as they emerge and treat them all as guests from whom to grow and learn. Only after embracing our feelings can get work in our garden to nurture positive seeds and transform seeds of affliction. For example, if we learn to acknowledge fear as a sprout, we can transform it before it arises and takes deep root.

> *Breathing in, I am aware of my fear.*
> *Breathing out, I embrace my fear.*

Perceptions

Our thoughts are so powerful that they can quickly turn into ideas or judgments about self and others. By stopping, calming and looking deeply, we can recognize when these perceptions are not accurate. One of my favorite practices is to ask, "Am I sure?"

Can you recall a situation in which you created a view about something or someone that turned out to be totally false? Such perceptions begin with thoughts that then become distorted. I recall receiving a beautiful needlepoint as a gift from our sister-in law following a family vacation on the coast. We placed it prominently in our home as a constant reminder of our wonderful time together.

Several months later, we mentioned how many beautiful memories were evoked by the needlepoint. She asked, "Did you notice the blemish in the corner?" So often our mind overlooks the overall beauty and goes directly to the tiny flaw, which is rarely noticed.

Perceptions often become deceptions because of our natural tendency to get caught on the negative, while positive perceptions disappear like the proverbial water off a duck's back. With mindfulness as my guide, I am able to step back and witness the rational or irrational nature of my ongoing perceptions. This practice helps me gain a clear understanding of what is taking place in this moment. It reminds me of standing, as I did recently, by the side of an ocean inlet on a still evening. The mountains behind me were beautifully mirrored in water's surface, reflecting what is true and what is real.

> *Breathing in, I am aware of my current perceptions.*
> *Breathing out, am I sure?*

Mental Formations: The Stories of Our Lives

As we explore the qualities of the present moment, we realize that our perceptions of our experiences are formed over time. Gardens are physical formations that have been nurtured over the years and shaped by myriad conditions—sun, moon, rain, soil, compost and numerous seeds. Similarly, our bodies are shaped by countless conditions from the time of our birth, and our ever-changing feelings are molded by our experiences and interactions until they become mental formations.

A friend recently shared the challenges he had with his father during childhood. His father became angry easily, and my friend wondered if he had that same potential for anger. Our discussion turned to mindfulness, and by looking deeply he began to see that the seeds of his father's anger were also in him. He recalled becoming easily angered by insignificant events, and how similar his actions were to his father's. The father's anger watered the same seeds in the son, allowing them to grow deep and, under certain conditions, to erupt many years later.

Mental formations are the stories we create from our experiences. Perhaps they start with a physical pain, which leads to feelings and perceptions or anxiety or fear. We replay these stories in the middle of the night when we are unable to sleep, each similar to a piece of music that continues to play repeatedly in our minds. Like a snowball rolling down a mountain, the faster it rolls, the larger it becomes.

In Buddhism there are fifty-one mental formations stored in the soil of our consciousness as seeds. These include feelings, perceptions, and wholesome and unwholesome seeds. When these seeds are triggered by an experience or event, they spring up in the mind or garden of our consciousness as a mental formation. For example, in the soil of my consciousness, the seed of fear lies dormant alongside many other seeds, such as awareness and faith. When I experienced the back spasms, I became aware of the seed of fear in my mind consciousness. Using mindfulness, I was able to recognize that the fear in that moment was related not only to the pain, but also to all my previous experiences of fear.

Breathing in, I am aware of my favorite mental formation or story.
Breathing out, I embrace that story.

Consciousness

The final pathway leading us deeply into the present moment is consciousness, which includes the mind consciousness (the visible garden) and the store consciousness (the soil and seeds). Every experience in our lives has influenced the seeds in our consciousness. Every time we water or give attention to one or another, we create a story or mental formation, and that seed becomes active in our mind consciousness. The longer we keep the seed alive in our mind, the stronger its roots become in our soil consciousness. For example, the longer I am angry with someone, the more likely I am to remain angry and to become angry more often. This explains why a person may erupt violently after a minor situation—the current anger is a manifestation of all the anger that was experienced and stored in the past.

Just as a garden needs a variety of elements to grow, so does a beautiful, vibrant life. It is a process of cultivating our store consciousness, which includes soil, seeds and compost.

Having developed our practice of mindfulness, we can more easily observe the seeds that lie deep within our consciousness, and learn how to water or transform these seeds and how to aerate the soil so there is healthy circulation between the soil and garden of our consciousness, the store and mind consciousness. You will soon discover how the quality of your life depends on which seeds you have watered and have allowed others to nurture throughout your life.

> *Breathing in, I am aware of the seeds that make up*
> *the quality of my life.*
> *Breathing out, I embrace all of my seeds.*

Practice:

- Find a comfortable place that allows for complete relaxation with no interruptions, and create an opportunity to become aware of your immediate environment. Ask yourself the following:

  > What am I seeing …colors, shapes, beauty?
  > What am I hearing… birds, people, cars?
  > What is happening in my body at this moment: type of breathing. tension in my muscles, pain, and state of relaxation?

- What feelings are the most challenging to be with?
- Reflect on a person or situation that you are struggling with and ask the question, "Am I sure?"

- What stories continue to play in your mind? Can you unearth the origin of these stories or mental formations?
- What positive qualities or seeds were watered in your life?

Take a moment to find a comfortable position and become aware of your breathing. As you do so, say to yourself...

> *Breathing in, I am aware that I am breathing in.*
> *Breathing out, I am aware that I am breathing out.*
> *Breathing in, I hear the sound of the birds.*
> *Breathing out, I smile.*
> *Breathing in, I am aware of tension in my body.*
> *Breathing out, I release my tension.*
> *Breathing in, I am aware of the preciousness of this day.*
> *Breathing out, I vow to live deeply in this day.*

CHAPTER 5

Exploring the Garden of Our Consciousness

"The quality of our life depends on the quality of the seeds that lie deep in our consciousness." —*Thich Nhat Hanh*

As we develop our skills as master gardeners, we become deeply aware of how the quality of our lives is influenced by the seeds that have been watered. Everything that affects our consciousness enters metaphorically as a seed. The master gardener serves as gatekeeper and protector of the consciousness. According to Thich Nhat Hanh, "Our mind is a field, in which every kind of seed is sown—seeds of compassion, joy and hope, seeds of sorrow, fear and difficulties." Seeds refer to all the emotions and qualities that enter our awareness and get stored in our consciousness. Using this awareness, think of a typical day. What seeds or feelings are you allowing to enter your consciousness through the media, the people in your life, and your everyday conversations? For parents and those who tend to the well-being of others, how do we protect the consciousness and precious potential of the human gardens in our care?

Previous generations cultivate life's seeds and pass them on through interactions with family, friends and the world around them. From the time we're born, these seeds are nourished. They grow through every interaction and transform through mindfulness in every season of our lives. A grandmother's happiness watered the seed of happiness in her daughter, who in turn nourishes that seed in her unborn child. A grandfather's anger watered the same seed in his son, who continued with his own children. The process of sowing, watering, nourishing, and cultivating the seeds of consciousness is an integral part of the life cycle supporting a healthy or unhealthy lineage. Mindful parents learn to rely on being happy and peaceful, transmitting the best gift we can give to our children.

Like all living things, seeds go through cycles of birth and death. A cherry pit has the potential to produce a cherry tree—and eventually more fruit and seeds. All seeds require the proper conditions to manifest, just as a garden needs nutrients in order for plants to grow. Master gardeners apply their skills to the seeds that need watering (loving-kindness, joy, compassion and equanimity) and the seeds to be transformed (anger, fear, jealousy and doubt) to develop a beautiful garden.

Through the seed metaphor we can deeply explore some of the causes and conditions that influence personal growth and development. "Seed language" is comparable to developmental psychology, which centers on the characteristics and changes that occur with time and maturity. Among the various lexicons used to describe relationships, seed language offers an overview similar to the "love languages" popularized by Dr. Gary Chapman. He suggests that each person has their own "language" to demonstrate love which includes: words of affirmation, quality time, receiving gifts, acts of service and physical touch. In a similar way, learning which seeds to water in ourselves and how to selectively water those seeds in others is the basis of understanding and love.

Mind and Store Consciousness

Our store consciousness or the unconscious mind is everything below the soil, our mind consciousness is everything above the soil. The garden illustrates the concept of the seeds being below the soil, in the store consciousness, and the flowers and weeds being above the soil, in the mind consciousness. Whatever we experience is a manifestation of our awareness of the present moment filtered through our mind consciousness. For example, this spring I was sitting on the shoreline of a small pond in a park, and I jotted down everything I was aware of:

> *I am aware of the blossoming trees, the warm sun on my back, and a variety of sounds, sights, and smells. I stop and take a few breaths. I am aware of a cacophony of birds and the sound of a meandering stream cascading down some rocks in the distance. I am aware of some chatter and movement in the bushes behind me of small birds rustling through the dried leaves. The radiating sun warms my body.*

Mind consciousness is present moment awareness—this is a beautiful day. Occasionally my mind drifted to happy experiences in my childhood, playing in nature. In that intimate moment, I was aware of my thoughts, feelings, body and the story I was creating about the moment, including how quickly I reflected on similar stories or experiences from the past. The environment and my peace of mind activated memories in my store consciousness, which is also known as the root consciousness—an appropriate name to represent the place where all the seeds are stored in our garden.

Seeds of Suffering and Seeds of Love

Seeds of consciousness fall into two distinct categories—seeds of love and seeds of suffering. Consider what happens when we witness or experience someone's anger, hatred, violence, abuse, jealousy or craving. The behavior is first noted in our mind consciousness. Immediately thoughts, feelings and perceptions arise and cause us to create a mental formation or story. We then experience this story in our mind consciousness—the part of the garden that we see—which simultaneously triggers a response in our store consciousness, underground. When the "seeds of affliction" are experienced

Mind

Mindfulness

Store

or watered, our typical response is to avoid or suppress them by pushing them deep into the store consciousness. The same holds true when the seeds of love are experienced or nurtured. We don't suppress them, but we do allow them to take root in our store consciousness. Thus we must become aware of and water the positive seeds of love and embrace and transform the negative seeds and afflictions that have been suffered.

Over the years, my experience as a prison volunteer has taught me how the seeds of affliction can dramatically impact a person's life and happiness. In the prison I visit, one of the inmates (JR) is serving a life sentence with no chance of parole. Living in the small Intensive Management Unit with nearly twenty other inmates, he is constantly bombarded by the collective seeds of suffering that have been planted in the store consciousness of his "cellies." During his own early years, the seeds of suffering—primarily anger, jealousy, fear, hate and violence—were watered by an abusive family, alcohol and drug abuse, and numerous attempts to assert himself in destructive ways. The soil and conditions for his life were already primed at an early age.

Unlike this inmate, some children grow up in a family where love abounds and where they are nurtured and held by parents who recognize the importance of positive interactions for their beloved child. The seeds of joy, love, compassion and peace are visible in such families. Every smile is a celebration, every cry an opportunity for compassion, and the overall home environment is peaceful. Family and friends support this child in loving ways. At school she is surrounded by other loving people who truly see her as a miracle and fortify her positive attributes or seeds. Her parents take time to "be" with her and convey that she is valued and important. It is easy to imagine what this child's life will be like as she grows and learns. With such an upbringing, she will be less inclined to stealing, violence and/or self-medicating to avoid the pain of life.

Despite the horrific life my prison friend experienced, he writes to me and shares that his mindfulness meditation practice has been a saving grace, a refuge to cope with the ongoing violence and verbal assaults that take place in the prison environment. He continues to transform the seeds of affliction on a daily basis through his meditation and understanding of how to cultivate the garden of his consciousness. In a recent letter, he wrote, "Cultivate peace in the garden of your heart by removing the weeds of selfishness and jealousy, greed, anger, pride and ego. Then all will benefit from your peace and harmony."

I often pause to reflect on the seeds that have been watered to lead me to this place in time, in which I have the opportunity to share these ideas. Likewise, I have learned through my own difficulties the importance of transforming the seeds of affliction that arise from my store consciousness. In every moment, I recognize that I have choices regarding the people with whom I interact, the materials I read, the programs I watch on television and video, and the music I play.

Looking Deeply at Consumption

Our practice of "watering the wholesome seeds" begins with an awareness of our consumption. We need food for survival and for well-being, yet our consumption is often based on some unmet need or a desire to feel good. Overeating may easily cause feelings of regret as well as irrational perceptions or mental formations about who we are and our worth as a person. We note this experience in our mind consciousness, and the longer it stays in our awareness, the deeper it takes root in our store consciousness. Learning to guard the garden of our consciousness is the best preventive medicine for both physical and emotional well-being.

One way to transform at the root level is to be mindful of the overall impact of what, why and how we consume. What we consume entails much more than food and drink, and unmindful consumption leads to suffering. This awareness helps us realize that the psychological nutrients we consume affect our ability to love and be happy.

Reflection on Mindfulness Training:
Unmindful Consumption

"Aware of the suffering caused by unmindful consumption, I am committed to cultivating good health, both physical and mental, for myself, my family, and my society by practicing mindful eating, drinking, and consuming. I will practice looking deeply into my consumption of the Four Kinds of Nutriments—edible foods, sense impressions, volition, and consciousness" —Thich Nhat Hanh

Such awareness creates the correct nourishment, healing support, and ethical grounds for living. Consuming negativity—such as violent movies and sexually explicit materials—waters the seeds of suffering, influencing thoughts, feelings, perceptions, mental formations and consciousness as well as my ability to love and be happy. My personal practice is to protect my consciousness by nurturing the seeds of love and happiness while limiting contamination of my consciousness, which has the potential to activate the seeds of suffering. As master gardeners, our practice must be to protect the consciousness of others, especially the fragile gardens of children and of those we love.

As you have explored the deepest part of your garden, you have discovered the causes and conditions in the form of the seeds that brought you to this place. You may have remembered seeds that have created suffering. You also discovered positive seeds, together with the various gardeners who watered those seeds in you. As a child, you often had little choice as to what seeds were watered. Now, with mindfulness, you can begin to make choices as to what you consume and what seeds to nurture or transform.

Take time to stop, be calm and look deeply at the seeds in the garden of your consciousness. Your happiness today depends on the seeds of suffering and the seeds of love that have been stored throughout your life.

Practice:

Find a quiet space and bracket a period of time during which you can reflect on the following questions:

- What positive seeds brought you to this place in time? What specific seeds were watered that demonstrated to you that you were and are loved?
- What seeds have challenged you in your life and contributed to your pain and suffering? Look deeply at the seeds of anger, violence and fear, for example, without blame or judgment of yourself or others.
- Look deeply at the seeds of love. What qualities were watered that have established you as a loving person today?
- Look deeply at the seed of fear. What experiences and qualities were watered that established this seed in your consciousness today?

CHAPTER 6

Watering Seeds of Love and Transforming Seeds of Suffering

"I give life to that which I notice. What I don't notice dies."
—Virginia Satir

Having explored the garden of our consciousness and reflected on and examined the seeds that have been most influential in our personal growth, we can now turn our attention to illustrations of and suggestions for watering seeds of love and transforming seeds of suffering in our lives.

I often pause to reflect on the influential gardeners who tilled the soil of my being, watering seeds within me based on their own personal life's journey and the seeds that had been watered within them—their own hopes, dreams, needs and challenges. I easily recall individuals who cared, supported and watered seeds of joy, kindness and the desire to serve within me, as well as those who watered worry, fear and judgment. Some of their efforts are reflected in the way I live my life today. There are times when this process of watering and transforming seeds happens randomly, since not all of our behavior is informed by conscious awareness.

The seeds of achievement and success were nurtured in my brothers and me by parents who grew up in the aftermath of the Great Depression. They also watered seeds of compassion, frugality and uncertainty. For example, my fear of not having enough influenced my relationship to money and my reluctance to buy things even though I might need them. Teachers and professors planted and inspired the seeds of optimism and hope and supported me in choosing a career that would encourage my gifts for deep sharing and listening, mentoring and service. A favorite professor, Dr. Don Willie, ignited the spark of my potential and positive qualities through his teaching and selective watering of my desire to learn, teach and be compassionate toward others. His belief in others created a positive self-fulfilling prophecy and belief that, regardless of background or circumstances, anyone could find and develop their true potential. His unconditional support and belief in me helped me as well as the multitude of students I worked with throughout my career.

While my parents watered the seeds of achievement and success in my brothers and me, they also—having grown up in a difficult period in this nation's history—watered seeds of compassion as well as of uncertainty and thrift. My teachers and professors planted and inspired the seeds of optimism and hope and supported me in choosing a career that would develop my gifts of deep sharing and listening, mentoring and service.

Spiritual teachers offered and continue to offer guidance and direction on my inner journey, including Thich Nhat Hahn, teacher, who inspired me to "water the seeds of love through [my] teaching and writing," as I endeavor to do today.

My spouse and I remain committed to watering the seeds of loving-kindness, tenderness, compassion and understanding in our relationship, as well as to the process of transforming the seeds of adversity that are an inevitable part of life's journey together. Over the years we have become more open to discovering the truth of each moment as we water and transform the seeds of our consciousness, as individuals and as a couple.

As all parents do, I tried to water the seeds of joy, affection and laughter in my son and daughter as they grew, although I can now look back and see that my efforts did not include watering the seeds of patience and presence. At that time, the seed of presence had not yet been deeply watered or nurtured in me, and my children often became my gardeners, the young bells of mindfulness reminding me to stop skipping pages when reading bedtime stories. From them I learned to stop and listen deeply, and to be there for them as I recalled the power of their beginner's minds.

Later, prompted by a lifetime of hurry sickness and a stressful lifestyle, in mid-life I sought and found a new seed—mindfulness—to plant, water and slowly cultivate in the core of my consciousness. Learning mindfulness was, for me, the centerpiece of my garden and ultimately of all my relationships.

Our gardens hold a myriad of seeds watered in our lifetime—certain ones seeming to cling like thorns and others shining brightly as sunflowers. Most of my life has been happy and filled with opportunity, but behind the scenes of my drive and success, the seed of doubt, of feeling "not enough," has often surfaced and has been a driving force for my habit energy to work harder and harder. With this awareness, I now ask, "Why am I doing this? Is it because of my passion or desire to be noticed and feel 'enough?'" Today, when such feelings arise, I am aware that I have choices to accept or reject outdated messages that are not loving or accepting, to understand my motives, and to replace them with more affirming self-talk focusing on life well lived and the truth in this moment, I am enough and do not need to prove myself time and time again.

"When we learn to stop and be truly alive in the present moment, we are in touch with what's going on within and around us. We aren't carried away by the past, the true, our thinking, ideas, emotions and projects." —Thich Nhat Hanh

GARDENING GUIDELINES

As master gardeners our goal in life is to create a beautiful garden, one that begins by understanding how to select the best seeds, how to plant and water, and how to have faith that what we have planted will grow. As parents, we help our children make good choices so that negative seeds watered by friends and media do not harmfully influence them. Sometimes weeds need to be removed and fences or boundaries created to protect the young buds so that they may grow in healthy ways.

In all our relationships, we must learn how to limit exposure to negative seeds such as fear, anger, jealousy and feelings of doubt. Meanwhile, we also learn how to support positive qualities such as gratitude, generosity, loving-kindness, joy and compassion. Sometimes we are required to weed out the harmful qualities and find other seeds that enrich the soil of our consciousness and relationships.

Several gardening guidelines will help bring this model to life and prepare us for the journey of watering the seeds of love in ourselves and others.

Keep the Doors to the Heart and Mind Open

When we begin to explore the wonders of the present moment, we almost naturally begin to stop and become calmer. Then we can begin to discover all the gifts the moment has to offer, tapping into our bodies, feelings, and perceptions, and thus keeping the metaphorical door between our mind and store consciousness open. When we are open to what is arising in our mind and store consciousness, we can dive deeply beneath the surface and bring to light the life stories that so often trigger emotions that cause us to respond in mindless, unconscious ways. We develop a new awareness of the connection between what is happening in the moment and what has happened in the past, allowing us to make conscious choices and live the fullness of life.

When I experience the feeling of anger in the present moment, I recognize that this feeling has been formed over a period of time and is not simply connected with the current situation. It is often related to what I had stuffed and stored in the ground of my consciousness. When you can make a healthy connection between what is happening in the moment and what has happened in the past or elsewhere in your life, you create the ideal condition for psychological well-being.

Keeping the door open means being open to all that is arising in the present moment. When suffering from the past rears its painful head, I often revert to my old habit of keeping busy to avoid those stressful feelings. Being open can be especially difficult when those we love are suffering. Our tendency is to want to change their feelings or try to fix the problem. While we intend those efforts to be loving, the deepest form of love is to be there, allow the feelings to arise in our beloved, and not attempt to change or control what they are feeling. To love is to water the seeds of deep listening, compassion, and unconditional love. And to do so, the doors to the mind and heart must remain open.

Don't Give Negative Seeds a Chance to Blossom

Our next step is to reorganize our lives to minimize the influence of negative seeds. The longer a seed is watered in the mind consciousness, the more likely it will become a mental formation and thus reinforce a story that then becomes deeply rooted in the store consciousness. Allowing such seeds to take root can be crippling. For example, I know fear develops in me the more I worry about completing a task. The longer I focus on fear, the more deeply rooted it becomes, overwhelming me and preventing me from getting the job done.

Negative seeds such as anger, fear, jealousy and doubt often lie just beneath the surface, waiting for an invitation to emerge and become active. One spark can easily start a major forest fire in the mind and heart. By practicing mindfulness, we can more easily become aware of the "extreme fire conditions" that activate those seeds and, through this awareness, quiet them.

To keep negative seeds dormant, we should reexamine what activities and relationships most influence our feelings of happiness or feelings of suffering. We should recall that feelings are generated after being exposed to the variables, or potential triggers, that water negative seeds. One way to minimize triggers that evoke negative seeds is to surround yourself with friends who recognize your positive qualities. The Celts honor a concept called "Anam Cara" or soul friend—a person who accepts us unconditionally. In seed language, such a person helps us get in touch with the beautiful seeds within and disarm the triggers that influence our negative seeds.

Another way to control the influence of negative seeds is to be aware of your consumption. In this technologically advanced world with its 24/7 connectivity, we have countless stimulants to entertain and to feed our hunger for information and connection. By reducing your media consumption, especially media that is violent in nature, you may discover, as I have, that you experience less anxiety in daily life. This does not mean I close my eyes to the world or to suffering. I can be compassionate without being preoccupied by media reports. Personally, I have made a commitment to avoid consuming violence in any form since this is high-octane fuel for igniting negative seeds. Violence is especially harmful to our children. It often prompts unhealthy models for conflict resolution, it desensitizes young people to violent acts, and it has watered thousands of seeds of suffering.

It is impossible to control all of life's circumstances and avoid contact with every negative seed. Even accidental encounters may trigger feelings that were previously stored, especially if those feelings have not been transformed. Regardless of how ideal your childhood was or how positive your relationships are today, you still carry negative seeds that were planted in the past and continue to influence your life and relationships.

Consider the following strategies for transforming these seeds:

RETURN TO THE PRESENT MOMENT

Similar to seed consciousness is Eckart Tolle's concept of "pain body," which he defines as a "collection of all the pain, misery, and sorrow a person has ever gone through their entire life, and all the things that are inherited from their culture and family history as well." According to Tolle, the only way to minimize the impact of this suffering is to return to the present so that the mind no longer needs to identify with the collective pain being experienced. Thus, practicing mindfulness and fully experiencing the present moment is the ideal way to counter the seeds of suffering as they arise.

MINDFUL BREATHING

By inviting mindfulness into our awareness and through the practice of mindful breathing, our focus is naturally changed, and our body and mind become more relaxed.

> *Breathing in, I am aware of my in breath.*
> *Breathing out, I am aware of my out breath.*
> *Breathing in, I am aware of this beautiful day.*
> *Breathing out, I smile.*

CHANGE THE MUSIC

The Buddha referred to "changing the peg," which was a metaphor derived from observing the way furniture was repaired more than 2,600 years ago. When a piece of furniture broke at a joint, it was repaired by changing the peg between the two joining pieces of wood, replacing the weak, broken peg with one that was strong and whole. A more contemporary metaphor would be to change the music to something that is more relaxing or pleasing and change our focus to something more affirming and positive.

The classic prayer of St. Francis of Assisi has always moved me. Each line can be an affirmation to help change the peg or the music:

> *Lord, let me be an instrument of thy peace.*
> *Where there is hatred, let me sow love;*
> *Where there is injury, pardon;*
> *Where there is doubt, faith;*
> *Where there is despair, light;*
> *Where there is sadness, joy.*

Give Positive Seeds a Chance to Blossom

One of the joys of relationships is to cultivate in others their own desire to recognize and support the positive qualities in themselves and others. Every time we recognize a child's positive behavior, that seed becomes stronger in their mind and forms deep roots in the soil of the store consciousness.

Several years ago, my wife took our young nephew to a popular Portland bookstore. His father had given him some additional money to spend at the bookstore, and he was very excited about the visit. On the way to the store, they passed an alcove where a homeless man lay on his sleeping bag. My nephew asked why he was there, and my wife explained that he had no home. Without prompting or encouragement, our nephew simply walked over to the man and placed his spending money near the sleeping bag. It was a powerful example of how his parents had watered the seeds of compassion and generosity in his young life.

We may find it helpful to organize our day to maximize the opportunities for positive seeds to emerge—spending time in nature, where the seeds of joy and beauty emerge together with peace and serenity, being with affirming and nurturing friends who influence our positive seeds to actively flourish and take deeper root. How different our relationships would be if we took time each day to recognize and shine light on the beautiful qualities within each other!

"Recognize the positive seeds in the person you love, water those seeds, and he will become much happier." —Thich Nhat Hanh

If we learn to mindfully arrange our lives so that positive seeds are touched many times each day, we will optimize our well-being and the quality of the relationships we have with those we love. The longer we can hold those positive mental formations in our mind consciousness, the more we strengthen the base or store consciousness.

Practice:
- Take a journey back in time and create a map of your psychological garden, illustrating the seeds of love and seeds of suffering that have brought you to this place in your life. Take time to offer gratitude to those on whose shoulders you now stand.
- Explore ways in which you might water the seeds of loving-kindness, compassion, joy and equanimity. (It's fine to look ahead in this book for more clarity regarding these seeds.)
- Reflect on ways to apply mindfulness practice to transforming the seeds of suffering including fear, worry, anger, inadequacy, jealousy and craving.
- Examine whether you spend more time watering the seeds of love or the seeds of suffering in a typical day.

*If you trace problems in your relationship
back to the beginning,
You will find their seeds
were sown and then ignored.
They grew unnoticed until their fruit
ripened and surprised you.
But if you can find
where the seeds were sown,
there you will find the roots as well.*

And if you remove the roots,
your problem will wither.
                    —William Martin

CHAPTER 7

Mantra Practice

*"Whatever you frequently dwell on, to that
the mind will be inclined."*   —*The Buddha*

On some level, we are all probably aware that what we focus on will manifest in our everyday life. Through a process called mantra practice, you will discover how to set your intention and manifest what you truly desire by watering the positive seeds in yourself and in your relationships.

What are mantras?

According to Thich Nhat Hanh, "a mantra is a magic formula that, once it is uttered, can entirely change a situation, our mind, our body or a person. But this magic formula must be spoken in a state of concentration—that is to say, a state in which body and mind are absolutely in a state of unity."

Mantras are not new. All world religions have some proscribed process of calming the mind—meditation, reflection, contemplation, chanting, prayer. Psychologists and spiritual teachers espouse the use of positive affirmations, which are another form of mantra. Spiritual teacher Louise Hay tells us that affirmations are a means of directing your thoughts and thinking to maintain a positive outlook, saying, "They are like little reminder notes to the inner-self." In seed language, they are a means of staying focused on the positive seeds in our consciousness.

Mantras help us to unify mind and body through the repetition—verbally or non-verbally—of words, sounds or short phrases. This repetitive practice becomes a waking meditation, gradually helping us to stop, be calm, and focus on what is important in the moment, making it possible to water the seeds of love in a more conscious way.

Mantra, a Sanskrit word, can be divided into two parts—"manas" meaning the mind and "tra" meaning tool. Mantras are a tool to exercise the mind, and by using them on a regular basis, we strengthen our ability to nurture the seeds and relationships we desire. One way to water the appropriate seeds is to first determine what seeds need cultivating and then to create a mantra practice to strengthen that seed quality within both the mind and store consciousness.

Value of Mantras

Mantras can become a powerful tool for us as we learn to water the seeds of love in ourselves and others. Life continually challenges our ability to be present, to focus, to meditate, to pray. The mind, frequently plagued by worrisome thoughts and endless chatter, can seem like a monkey continually jumping from tree to tree. It is no accident that Buddhists call this "monkey mind," and it reflects one of our greatest challenges as gardeners. Mantras can help us find refuge in quiet spaces within our consciousness that are often filled with mindless distractions. Practicing mantras reduces overall stress and infuses our consciousness with the messages that positively influence body, mind and spirit.

For example, studies have shown that Catholics reciting the rosary or a stream of Ave Maria's regulated their blood pressure, heart rate, and respiration in healing ways. Buddhists reciting the well-known mantra "Om Mani Padme Hum" had similar results. All of these repetitive expressions appear to create self-regulation that positively affects the immune system, the reduction of inflammation, and the regulation of blood sugar levels.

Dr. Herbert Benson, a pioneer in introducing meditation to the practice of medicine, found that any type of meditation had a positive physiological influence. However, those with a spiritual or religious background may find that words selected from that background support the motivation for using them. For example, Christians may find quoting favorite Bible verses or saying the "Centering Prayer" promoted by Basil Pennington to be a valuable means of redirecting their focus away from negative seeds, while Buddhists may find phrases such as "I am filled with loving-kindness" effective in focusing. The more personal the meaning attached to the mantra, the more successful it appears to be.

Creating Your Own Mantra Practice: Belief and Repetition

In creating a mantra, it is important to begin with a word or phrase that has personal meaning. In addition, for this and any practice to be effective, we must believe this practice will have a positive influence. Next, we must repeat the word or phrase many times to redirect our focus away from the stressors of life to the qualities that are important in our lives—thus infusing the positive seeds in the soil of our consciousness.

> *"When you speak with 100 percent of your being, your speech becomes mantra. In Buddhism, a mantra is a sacred formula that has the power to transform reality. You don't need to practice mantras in some foreign language like Sanskrit or Tibetan. You can practice in your own beautiful language. For if your body and mind are unified in mindfulness, then whatever you say becomes a mantra."*
> —Thich Nhat Hanh

Mantra Practice:
- Select a phrase that has personal and/or spiritual or religious significance to you. "Hail Mary" or the "Our Father," "God,"

"Om," "Allah," "Peace," "Love" are some examples. Ideally the words should resonate for you and offer you peace and generate loving-kindness.

- As in any formal meditation practice, find a comfortable position and begin to focus your attention on your breathing as you verbally or non-verbally repeat the word(s) or phrase you have selected. When your mind wanders, bring your awareness back to your breath and the word or phrase—again and again. Continue this in a comfortable position for 10-20 minutes. Through daily meditative practice you are learning to stop and calm yourself while watering the seeds that will nurture and support your journey.

Mantras can be used formally, as in sitting or praying, or as a means of practice in our ongoing interactions with those we love. For example, when we are with someone we love, they become the focus of our meditation or prayer. To ground me in the present moment when I am with another, I might say to myself, "I am here for you."

Selective Watering and Mantra Practice

Learning to love requires an understanding of our beloved and ourselves. When we understand another, we will know what messages will reinforce our relationships with them. As you will discover, there are a myriad of seeds, some of which need more attention than others. Each person is unique, and there is not one "love map" or seed planting guide that works for all.

Now that we have focused on understanding the practices of the gardener, we will turn our focus to examining the various seeds of consciousness, chapter by chapter. For each seed, such as compassion, I will suggest a mantra as a means of bringing this practice alive in your daily life. As you become familiar with this practice and the more you understand the seeds in those you love, you will find your own ways to focus your mindfulness and develop your mantra practice to nurture the seeds that need attention.

Enjoy the journey. May you find ways to become a master gardeners for yourself and all the relationships in your life.

Practice:
- As you start the practice of selective watering, review the chart of seeds in Chapter 5 and decide which seeds need to be watered or transformed in your life. Discovering which positive seeds need attention and which negative seeds cause suffering is a powerful way to begin this practice.
- Focus on one seed and create a mantra to help support you in the watering or reinforcement of this quality(ies) in yourself and those you love. For example, I find it is naturally easier to be with those I love when they are happy and positive. Yet true love means also being with them when they are hurting as well. During such times, I strive to water the seed of compassion by repeating the mantra, "I am here for you and my heart is open."

PART 3

Seeds Every Garden Needs

"A man asked the Buddha, 'What can I do to be sure that I will be with Brahma after I die?' And the Buddha replied, 'As Brahma is the source of Love, to dwell with him you must practice the Brahmaviharas—love, compassion, joy and equanimity.'"

—*Thich Nhat Hanh*

This section offers four chapters defining the qualities that are essential to all relationships—loving-kindness, compassion, joy and equanimity. In watering these primary seeds, you will discover the best ways to create the understanding necessary to know how best to love another. These seeds are often called "immeasurable" since, when watered and practiced, they can extend our personal love to the whole world. They are the answer to the question, "How can I best love you?"

With the practice of loving-kindness as the core, you will always have the best interest of others at the heart of your relationships. When loving-kindness is your strongest desire, you can support someone who is suffering by offering them compassion. With loving-kindness as an anchor, you celebrate in the joys of others. And when, despite your greatest desire to offer support, someone's suffering is beyond your reach, the best gift you can offer is equanimity, a calm and centered presence. As you can see, each of these core seeds are interrelated and dependent on one another. They are the cornerstones in the garden of all healthy relationships.

CHAPTER 8

Loving-Kindness

"My aspiration is to water the seed of loving-kindness in order to create understanding so that I can bring joy and happiness to my beloved and all beings." —*Thich Nhat Hanh*

Imagine living your life with the sole intention of making every interaction an opportunity for keeping the best wishes and goodwill of others foremost in your mind and heart. *Loving-kindness* is that intention—the capacity to offer joy, goodwill, and happiness to another.

Loving-kindness requires an ability to begin all our interactions by looking for the good in everyone we meet. Many years ago in Thailand, a monk saw a sparkle emanating from a crack in a clay Buddha statue. As he peeled away the clay, a large solid gold Buddha was found. Legend suggests that the monks hid the gold by camouflaging it with clay to prevent invaders from stealing the treasure. This story offers a reminder that what we are looking for is often hidden as a gem within.

Think of people who greet you with warmth and acceptance regardless of your mood or circumstance. They are beaming with the energy of loving-kindness—often easier to experience than to describe. When we think of the most loving person we know, we automatically smile because they project a joyful energy that in turn, waters joy within ourselves. Loving-kindness is open, spacious, and overflowing—not effusive or gushy, but sincerely joyful and tender. People who exemplify these qualities naturally share their appreciation, they are attentive to the needs of others, and they demonstrate a natural ability to be affectionate in caring ways.

In the wisdom traditions, loving-kindness has been purported to generate numerous personal benefits such as improved health and well-being, as well as the ability to experience love more deeply and intimately, since it allows us to project a radiance of the heart and mind. Loving-kindness is always practiced for the benefit of others, and because of our "Interbeing nature" the practice becomes mutually satisfying. Loving-kindness practice begins with an unconditional love and acceptance of self. As Sharon Salzberg said, "You can explore the universe looking for somebody who is more deserving of your love and affection than you are yourself, and you will not find that person anywhere."

Self love is different than being arrogant, egotistic or conceited. It is about respecting and honoring yourself and your own unique life's journey. Loving yourself requires knowing and taking responsibility for yourself. You are aware of your strengths and weaknesses and open to change and growth. Loving another is only fully possible when it grows from the seed of self love.

More than 2,600 years ago, the Buddha was practicing with his monks in the Jeta Grove in India during the rainy season. As was the tradition, the monks took temporary residence in the forest to engage in intensive meditation practice. Once there, however, the monks found themselves believing that "tree deities" were doing everything possible to scare them away from their place in the forest. Feeling harassed and fearful, they came to the Buddha and shared their angst. The Buddha taught them the practice of what he called "metta," or loving-kindness meditation, as an antidote to their fear. So they began radiating thoughts of love and peace to all, eventually letting go of their fears and abiding peacefully in the forest during their retreat. How often do we awaken in the middle of the night haunted by the deities of fear in the form of deadlines, projects and feelings of unworthiness? Watering the seed of loving-kindness in ourselves and others is a way to cultivate love and peace in our lives.

Practices to Develop Loving-kindness

UNDERSTAND WHO AND WHAT WE LOVE

Mindfulness is about remembering who we are, where we are and what we love. The practice of loving-kindness begins with an intention or direction for our love. Taking time to reflect on the questions "What do I love?" and "Who do I love?" will support the beginning of understanding how best to love.

There is no question about the love I have for my wife, but just saying the words is not enough. Reflecting upon her as the "who" I love encourages me to best understand her needs in order to offer her support and make her a focus of my life. "Did I water the seed of love in her today? Was I practicing loving-kindness in our interactions and communications? Or is the flower that is my love wilting?" In bringing your awareness and attention to what and who you love, your beloved blossoms because there is understanding.

We can apply similar practices in other areas of our life, such as the environment. Saying we love the planet is not enough. We must spend time learning what is needed for tending and supporting our environment so we know how best to preserve and nurture the planet we love.

BE LOVE

It is so easy to expect others to be loving and kind, but often the mutuality of this concept is forgotten. Learning to take care of self as of a parent, partner and co-worker demonstrates the kind of self-love that is necessary for renewal and well-being. When a parent takes time to nurture herself, she models a positive message of self care and love which cannot be replaced with words. Being a model or a messenger of loving-kindness is always the best way to ultimately receive love ourselves. Others are always drawn to the energy of loving kindness—a warm smile, words of appreciation, sweet attention and affection. Remember that, deep within, you are ultimately love itself.

Practice Metta

Metta, or loving-kindness, is something we should practice moment-by-moment as well as daily. We can offer the practice of loving-kindness to ourselves, someone we have empathy for, someone we are fond of, a neutral person, or even someone we find challenging in our life. We practice offering loving-kindness with the purpose of creating happiness in another as well as ourselves. It is the process of developing a kind and loving energy, which literally infuses our every interaction.

Several years ago, my wife and I began an evening practice of sharing metta with each other before sleep. Because of this, our sleep has become deeper and more restful. In our practice, we begin with ourselves:

> *May I be filled with loving-kindness.*
> *May I be free from suffering.*
> *May I find joy.*
> *May I be well.*
> *May I find peace.*

After directing these words and feelings of loving-kindness to ourselves, we then extend thoughts of loving-kindness to each other by repeating the above phrases, replacing the "I" with "you." We conclude by sending this loving-kindness to people we love and especially to those we know are struggling at the time.

Sometimes it seems easier to share loving-kindness with others than to remember to include ourselves in the process. Many of us grew up with the admonition that we must put others first, sometimes at the expense of loving ourselves. How is it possible to give to others what we have not nurtured in ourselves? Personally, I have discovered that practicing loving-kindness toward myself through meditation, quiet reflection, long walks, and above all, time with loved ones, for example, provides me more time and energy to give to others and, ultimately, everyone benefits.

PRACTICE KINDNESS

Finally, consider one simple practice that the Dalai Lama models in all of his interactions—kindness. With the intention and practice of kindness, everyone is reminded of their capacity to experience joy, goodwill and happiness. This is beautifully expressed in the words of a gentle song called "Kindness" sung by the monks in Plum Village, France, where Thich Nhat Hahn resides:

> "What is the greatest, what is the greatest, what is the greatest wisdom of all? What is the greatest, what is the greatest, what is the greatest wisdom of all? Kindness, Kindness—that is greatest wisdom of all."

At times when I have the privilege of officiating a wedding ceremony, I often share the following: The seed of loving-kindness is the foundation of your relationship. Listen deeply to yourself and each other so that your priority is always the goodwill and happiness of each other. In this process you will know best how to be there for each other and develop true love. As you practice loving-kindness, your life will be a natural outpouring of love—the foundation for a happy life.

Regardless of our spiritual background, may we always remember the words of the Dalai Lama when he says. "My religion is kindness." With this reminder, we learn to water the seed of loving-kindness through metta practice extended to every interaction. Whenever we offer joy and goodwill to another, the seed of loving-kindness grows. It begins with self, radiates to others and soon becomes boundless.

Mantras:

- Today, I stop to remember who and what I love.
- I aspire to understand others and support their growth.
- May I (you, others) be filled with loving-kindness.
- May I (you, others) find joy.
- May I (you, others) be well.
- May I (you, others) find peace.
- Today I will bring wishes of well-being and goodwill to every person I meet.

CHAPTER 9

Compassion

"In the face of suffering, no one has the right to turn away, not to see." —Elie Wiesel

Compassion arises from the boundless nature of love. If we are truly practicing the seed of loving-kindness, we want the best for others and want to relieve their suffering. When we say, "I love you," how is that translated in behaviors? Since love is a verb as well as a noun, some action is required. In everyday relationships, being there for another is more important than doing. When difficulties arise in relationships, the tendency is often to try to fix the problem. When we love someone, it is almost instinctual to try to find ways to make things better immediately. Yet the best response may be to just *be*, to listen, to offer our pres-

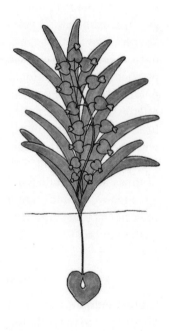

ence, and to demonstrate in words and behavior that nothing and no one is more important in this moment in time. In so doing we learn to understand how and why they are suffering—we are compassionate.

A time comes in all our lives when we are called to give love in more active ways. This can take the form of caring for an elderly parent or community volunteering, for example. Perhaps we are called upon to be there for another in a time of grief or personal tragedy. These are experiences that require more from us—more time, more energy, more resources. Our efforts, when offered in the spirit of loving-kindness, can serve to deepen our compassion and heighten our awareness of the unique journey of each of our fellow human beings.

Several years ago my wife and I accompanied a group of students on a pilgrimage to India. On this journey, and from the vantage point of an elevated tour bus, we were all deeply moved by a young girl, approximately six years old, with a severe facial deformity. We later learned that a large tumor, growing inside her mouth from birth, caused many challenges, especially malnutrition, as well as psychological burdens for her and her family. Our friend and fellow pilgrim, Rita, made it a point to find this child and her mother and offer assistance. After our journey, Rita began a program to help little "Muni," which involved many return trips to India to work with the health care system. As a result of fund-raising and advocacy, Muni could smile for the very first time in her life. Because of Rita's loving-kindness, the seed of compassion was watered in what is a worldwide community of friends who found ways to open their hearts to relieve suffering and offer a new life for this young woman in India.

Never Turn Away

On that journey, we learned one very important lesson—keep our hearts open to the suffering that exists and don't turn away. I have used that axiom to confront many challenges in my life. Sometimes it is my beloved who is suffering, or my son or daughter. Compassion is the ability to embrace that moment of pain. Sometimes it is a homeless person holding a sign, asking for money. Sometimes I give, sometimes I don't—yet I always strive to keep my heart open with what one Indian teacher calls a "glance of mercy." In that moment the seed of compassion is watered both in the other person and ourselves.

"You can hold yourself back from the sufferings of the world, that is something you are free to do, but perhaps this very holding back is the one suffering you could avoid. "   —Franz Kafka

What Is Compassion?

The derivation of compassion can be best understood when the word is divided into two parts: "com," which means "together with" and "passion," which means, "to suffer." True love has one primary purpose, and that is to help reduce and transform the suffering or pain of others. In Buddhism, the goddess figure Avalokiteshvara or Kwan Yin is known as a "bodhisattva," an archetypal figure representing someone who is "awake" to the suffering of others. It is said that she practices "looking with the eyes of compassion and listening deeply to the cries of the world." Watering the seed of compassion requires an openness and awareness of the cries of suffering and the willingness to be there for another without turning away. Mother Teresa once said, "It is easy to go to India and become aware of suffering, but suffering can also be found right next door."

"To develop compassion in ourselves, we need to practice mindful breathing, deep listening, and deep looking." —Thich Nhat Hanh

Compassion is the ability to be touched by the suffering that exists within self and others. This quality is nurtured by learning to be empathetic to or aware of the suffering. Through an empathetic understanding of another's suffering, we are able to look deeply and decide whether to become involved. If we decide to do so, what do we need to do to actively reduce their suffering? Compassion is a desire to alleviate the suffering in another—it is an active demonstration of "true love." I love you not merely by my words, I love you and I am here for you because I know you are in pain.

During the last ten days of my mother-in-law's life, we witnessed hospice nurses, CNAs, music therapists, social workers, and chaplains minister to her and to us. It was so beautiful to know that in providing end-of-life care, the caregivers were not trying to prolong her life. Rather, they sought to make every moment pain-free so she could let go. After nearly ten days of numerous compassionate acts, she finally let go and took her last breath. In observing these beautiful acts of compassion, that seed was watered in us, which allowed us to grieve. Observing acts of compassion nourished that quality, like a gentle rain, and it became deeply rooted in us and available for those who may be suffering in the future.

We nurture it when we allow ourselves to be open to it, as witnesses and as recipients. In observing compassionate actions we are inspired to continue or pass on those feelings to all we meet. The concept of "emotional contagion" verifies this—when you see a person or group acting in a certain way may catch and feel those same emotions

Psychologist David McClelland, in a classic study, that coined the term the "Mother Teresa Effect," discovered that students who watched a video of Mother Teresa caring for orphans in Calcutta were positively influenced. In this study Harvard students had significant increases in an immune system antibody. They also appeared to focus more on loving and being loved.[1] It appears that acts of compassion are capable of awakening compassion within us.

Coming from a place of wanting the best for others, I realize that my first role is simply to be present with an open heart and mind—allowing others to talk, witnessing rather than reacting, and

---

1. This study, titled "The effect of motivational arousal through films on Salivary Immunogobulin A," first appeared in *Psychology & Health*, Volume 2, Issue 1, 1988, pages 31-52

demonstrating by my loving presence by being there for them unconditionally. They know it is safe to share their pain and the challenging seeds that are emerging during those times. This knowledge allows the person to be congruent and supports a healthy circulation between the garden and soil—what they are experiencing now and what have they stored in their consciousness.

Practices to Develop Compassion

MINDFUL BREATHING

One of the best ways to be there for another is to return to your breath. To be present with others and ourselves—Breathing in, I am aware of this present moment. Breathing out, I embrace this moment. Breathing in, I am aware of the suffering in another. Breathing out, I embrace their suffering.

DEEP LISTENING

Reassure another by your presence that they are the most important person in that moment and that, regardless of what is said, you will not turn away. Deep listening is a powerful way to relieve suffering. I am here for you and, supported by the embrace of loving silence, I listen deeply.

LISTEN TO SELF

Allow yourself to recognize what is happening in your body, feelings and perceptions (thoughts) during these times: I am feeling sad, I am aware of my thoughts, I am feeling tension in my body. I return to my breathing so that I can be truly calm, and listen.

LOOK DEEPLY

Focus on what is being touched in you as you interact with another and try not to turn away from the pain that is emerging. Often someone's pain will touch something deep in you which is usually connected to some kind of unfinished business from the past. Use this as an opportunity to learn more about yourself.

Being compassionate toward others begins with compassion for self. Be open to the story of the person right in front of you, and continue to expand that feeling to those you know, those we will never meet, and to mother earth.

> *"If you want others to be happy, practice compassion;*
> *If you want to be happy, practice compassion."*
> —*The Dalai Lama*

Mantras:
- I know you are suffering, and that is why I am here for you.
- When suffering, I stop to embrace what I sense, think and feel, to be with what is.
- When there is suffering, I stop, breathe and keep my heart open.

CHAPTER 10

Joy

"Works of love are always works of joy." —*Mother Teresa*

Is there someone in your life who always leaves you feeling better than you were before you connected with him or her? Perhaps you were feeling despair or sadness, yet after some time in their presence, you felt lighter, grateful and even inspired. You found yourself smiling more, and these feelings lingered long after the connection. This is what it feels like to have the seed of joy watered within you.

Possibly you are that person— one who offers joy to all you meet, watering the beautiful qualities in another as if tending the most precious flowers in their garden. How might your life be different if you became the catalyst for offering joy to those you meet on a daily basis? How would this change your relationships with those you love? As the renowned spiritual philosopher Henri Nouwen says, "Joy does not simply happen to us. We have to choose joy and keep choosing it every day." I would add that we have to choose joy in every moment.

What is Joy?

In his classic book *Teaching on Love*, Thich Nhat Hanh defines joy as a feeling filled with peace and contentment. "We rejoice when we see others happy, but we rejoice in our own well-being as well. How can we feel joy for another person when we do not feel joy for ourselves? Joy is for everyone." He also writes, "True love always brings joy to ourselves and the one we love. If it does not bring joy, it is not true love." The seed of joy grows out of gratitude, hope and love. In joy you feel part of the flow of life; you feel a sense of connection. For most people, joy represents feelings of pleasure, delight, gladness, and aliveness.

Ideally joy should be a way of life and not just something that happens occasionally, when the circumstances are perfect. Martin Luther King Jr. understood this when he said; "If a man is called to be a street sweeper, he should sweep them as Michelangelo painted, as Beethoven composed music, as Shakespeare wrote his plays." Or, in other words, "Whatever you do, work at it with all your heart." (Colossians 3:23)

Buddha said, "We are formed and molded by our thoughts. Those whose minds are shaped by selfless thoughts give joy when they speak or act. Joy follows them like a shadow that never leaves them." Think of people in your life who personify joy in their daily work. It could be a server in your favorite restaurant or the person who smiles at you on the subway. Students in my university classes often spoke of a man who worked at a local supermarket. Despite the day or weather, he was always upbeat and full of light and joy. People would intentionally wait in his line to have him bag their groceries. Joy followed him like a shadow. Similarly, people will often reflect on the qualities the Dalai Lama personifies—his smile and overall feeling of joy. Everyone feels better when they are around him as he notices others and truly connects on a deep personal level.

Joy and Happiness

Often the words joy and happiness are used interchangeably. According to the Dalai Lama, "The very purpose of our life is to seek happiness." At first this may sound narcissistic or self-serving. However, he believes that the source of this happiness comes from a strong sense of contentment, regardless of whether or not we achieve what we are striving for. Most people seek contentment by striving to obtain everything they want, including the perfect body, mate, money, house and cars. The Dalai Lama in *The Art of Happiness* asks, "Does this work?" Instead, he prescribes a better method: "to want and appreciate what we have."

Joy is a vital seed to water in ourselves and our relationships. It is essential to intimate relationships and one of the main reasons others choose to be with us. Once a month I talk to my best college buddy on the phone. For nearly an hour we laugh, tease, banter and catch up on each other's lives in what always becomes a time filled with joy. Radiating joy is especially easy when those around us emanate this feeling.

On our daily journey there is an inexhaustible number of moments—opportunities to experience joy. On my early morning walk in the park, I breathe deeply as I look up at colorful clouds aglow from the morning sun. The more mindful I am, the more likely I am to experience joyful moments along the way. In seed language, the more each event is fully experienced by our body, through our feelings and registered within our mind consciousness, the deeper that event is registered and stored in our consciousness helping to sustain the feeling in the future. Looking back on each day, I am reminded how easy it is to be in such a hurry that we miss moments of joy. These moments, whether they are long or brief, happen only when we stop and calm.

"Am I not a man? And is not a man stupid? I'm a man. So I married. Wife, children, house, everything. The full catastrophe."
—Zorba the Greek

As with all the seeds, we must return to the present moment to experience, as Zorba the Greek says so well, the "full catastrophe" of life. Joy is much more meaningful, necessary and intense when we experience life fully—including the worry and sadness that are companions of us all. As we all know, our well-being is that much more gratifying after we have been sick. From a seed perspective, we cannot fully experience the seeds of love if we resist the seeds of suffering. Tara Brach, a Buddhist teacher said in a talk, "Joy arises when we are open to both sorrows and beauty. When we have a presence that opens to the wholeness and truth that life includes—that openness is joy. We do this by opening our hearts and mind to the present experience of life with mindfulness as our flashlight, our lens."

Practices to Develop Joy

Linger a little longer
Look around and see what is beautiful in your life. Experience those positive events a little longer—savor the moment! Gaze a little longer. Look deeply into the face of a child, spouse or friend. Truly stop and see the radiant sunset or full moon. I recall taking my son and daughter, when they were young children, up in the foothills to watch the moon rise on fall evenings. Can you think of times when you stopped and lingered in order to savor a moment with a loved one? The longer these moments of joy are experienced in our mind consciousness, the happier we will be and the more we will remember these moments.

Recognize what is happening within your body, your feelings, your thoughts and perceptions, and remind yourself that you are creating a wonderful story or mental formation that will linger on in your memory long beyond the actual event. This validates the work of Rick Hanson, a physician and researcher who, in his book *Buddha's Brain,* suggests that our minds have a bias toward clinging to negativity. When we savor and experience each moment, if for only a few seconds, we keep the experience alive longer in our mind consciousness. Hanson advises us to "imagine or experience that feeling entering deeply into your mind and body." When we do this, the feeling becomes deeply rooted in our store consciousness.

PRACTICE GRATITUDE

One of the best avenues to joy is gratitude. Look around and be grateful for what you have, and avoid worrying about what you think you need in order to be happy. Look around. What do you have to be grateful for—health, family, friends, livelihood, food and shelter? Those moments in which you allow gratitude to truly sink into your consciousness are moments that carry with them great joy.

For my wife's last birthday, I presented her with several seed packets. On each packet I wrote the name of a specific seed of love that I recognize in her. Since when she volunteers as a clown her name is "Daisy," I placed a note about the joy that I see in her on the packet of daisy seeds. We continued to smile at the daisies as they bloomed that summer.

MAY YOUR HAPPINESS AND JOY INCREASE

Teacher Jack Kornfield suggests that, similar to loving-kindness or metta practice, we can visualize someone we love experiencing a happy moment and feel his or her well-being. We may then repeat, as a mantra or prayer, "May your happiness and joy increase." We continue to focus on them while sending joy to our loved ones and others in need. This focus on joy, happiness, and concern for others both waters that seed in ourselves and creates a connection of joy and happiness with the other. This overcomes any stress or anxiety that we may be feeling and counters the negativity bias we often have.

"Joy is prayer, Joy is strength. Joy is love. Joy is a net of love by which you can catch souls." —Mother Teresa

Mantras:

- I bring joy to every person I meet.
- I extend my gaze and joyfully linger in each moment.
- I find joy in the full catastrophe of living.

CHAPTER 11

Equanimity

"Equanimity means nonattachment, nondiscrimination, even-mindedness, or letting go. You climb the mountain to be able to look over the whole situation, not bound by one side or the other."
—*Thich Nhat Hanh*

What would your life look like if you felt completely in love with others and free at the same time?—free to be who you are and able to flow with life's ups and downs, not caught up in the feeling that things should be a certain way? You would experience nondiscrimination, a state of liberation from the boundaries between yourself and others. You would be able to remain calm and centered, thus able to be non-reactive and open to understanding all sides. You would be independent, able to stand alone, yet not feel separate from  others. From this even-minded vantage point, you would be ready to support yourself and others. You would have learned how to let go and would not be disturbed by others despite how they may have treated you. This is the seed of equanimity.

According to Rick Hanson as noted in his book *Buddha's Brain*, "The word equanimity comes from Latin roots meaning "even" and "mind." With equanimity, what passes through your mind is held with spaciousness so you stay even-keeled and are not thrown off balance. The ancient circuitry of the brain is continually driving you to react one way or another—and equanimity is your circuit breaker." Like all seeds, equanimity is more than a word: it is a practice. Learning to be unswayed by the circumstances of life is at the heart of understanding this seed. To maintain equanimity is the essence of the practice of mindfulness.

> *Breathing in, I am aware of the waves in my life.*
> *Breathing out, I find my peaceful center amidst the challenges of the moment.*

When I think of challenges that people must endure, I am reminded of JR, the prison inmate I mentioned in Chapter 5. Of his meditation practice he says, "My practice is what keeps me alive." This is literally and metaphorically true since he resides with the toughest of inmates in the prison's intensive management unit. Reflecting on the concept of seeds, what would it be like living in a confined space where the ongoing dialogue is a constant deluge of negativity—a watering of fear, anger, craving and jealousy? As a result of his mindfulness practice, JR has learned to return to the present moment to witness rather than react to the ongoing verbal assaults.

JR made a powerful choice to take shelter in the present moment. He is learning how to become a refuge of peace within a circle of violence and danger. This way of being is exemplified by a story meditation teacher Tara Brach tells about the concept of *querencia*— a place in the bull ring, a comfort zone, where the bull feels absolutely safe and whole. The matador observes patterns to determine this zone and uses these insights to his advantage to finally attack and kill the bull in his safe place. The bull teaches us that all creatures seek refuge, both intrinsically and instinctively, in times of stress. We all have a place of wholeness and power that is within our core. It is a place of peace, where we can stop, be calm, and look deeply. With mindfulness we discover that, despite the demands of the situation, we do not always need to react and thereby increase the stress of existing turmoil.

Thich Nhat Hanh offers another view: "We shed all discrimination and prejudice, and remove all boundaries between ourselves and others." He writes, "In a conflict, even though we are deeply concerned, we remain impartial, able to love and to understand both sides." With this understanding we are able to see others as equal, without perception of superiority or inferiority. Being able to see each person with unconditional love allows him or her to be free.

In personal relationships it is essential to offer each other freedom. A part of our marriage commitment, my wife and I pledged to offer one another the freedom and support to grow on our spiritual paths. The greatest gift we can give our partners and loved ones is the invitation to become who they truly are, encouraging them to learn, to risk and go beyond the boundaries of self-imposed perceptions. Are we able to let go of our children—to whisper like the angel to the blade of grass, "Grow, grow"? Thich Nhat Hanh asks the question, "Dear one, do you have enough space in your heart and all around you?" If you can truly answer yes, it is clear that you have true love in your relationship.

Practices to Develop Equanimity

TAKE REFUGE

We all need a personal inner space of peace and safety, like birds seeking refuge, returning to a familiar place time and again. With mindfulness as our practice, our first place of refuge is to return to the present. "I have arrived, I am home in the here and in the now, I am solid, I am free." Each breath can be an opportunity to gather our energy and return to our real "home," which is within.

By letting go of the past and the future, I am able to be present in the here and now.

Using the practice of mindfulness mediation, discover the place within you where you can take refuge whenever you need to. For me, a personal refuge is simply taking a breath and returning to the present moment. I combine the breath with a mantra—Breathing in, I am aware that this moment is a gift. Breathing out, I am happy in this moment. Creating practices like this allows you to build a mindfulness tool kit—strategies not dependent on someone else, but based on staying with the experience of the moment. Finding your own refuge is the practice! Reflect on how the skills and concepts shared in this book offer you strategies that will support your ability to stay centered during the challenges you face on life's journey.

TRANSFORM HABIT ENERGY

Our tendency to react automatically when confronted with challenging people and stressful situations forms a "habit energy." We typically condition and armor ourselves with an automatic response rather than take on the stance of witness. Our response may often add to the angst of the moment and create more hostility. Are you aware of your response to indifference, harsh words and anger in others?

I recall times when friends or family shared some challenges they were facing in their life. My typical "habit energy" has been to try to fix things for them rather than to simply be there. While this may work for problems around the household, I am learning that, with people, it is better to listen and witness rather than react by trying to fix what may be broken in their life.

LET GO OF ATTACHMENTS

One of my favorite sayings is "Attachments are the root of all suffering." Typical attachments include our identity with our body image, people, career, material goods, thoughts, feelings and anything that causes us to create a solid view of how things are and should be. If I am attached to how I want another person to be, I will suffer and so will they. If I am attached to how I wish something to turn out, I will suffer if it does not turn out the way I want. If I am attached to being right, I will suffer when I turn out to be mistaken. Nature illustrates the philosophy that everything is impermanent, that we are always changing. Gardeners recognize that, despite seasonal preferences, a garden needs a variety of conditions in order to thrive. Through the garden metaphor, we understand that becoming attached to a flower, a season and or even a feeling is irrational.

Grasping anything too tightly can be costly. It is like the old story of the monkey trap, which has several variations. In a Southeast Asian version, hunters will trap monkeys by making a hole in a coconut, scraping out the inside, and placing a piece of candy in the hollow shell. Finding the coconut, the monkey reaches in to grasp the tasty treat. Once it grabs the candy, it makes a fist and holds on tightly. Unable to let go of the candy, the monkey's paw remains stuck, and the monkey becomes easy prey for the hunter. What are you grasping or holding on to?

"If you let go a little, you will have a little peace. If you let go more, you have more peace. And if you let go completely, whatever happens, your heart will be free."
– *Ajahn Chah (in Jack Kornfield's* The Wise Heart: a Guide to the Universal Teachings of Buddhist Psychology*)*

Mantras:
- In every challenging situation, I take a breath and return to my peaceful center.
- By letting go of my attachment to control, I stop to see both sides clearly.
- I let go of control so others can be free.

PART 4

The Seeds That Nourish Every Garden

Kind hearts are the gardens, kind thoughts are the roots,
kind words are the flowers, kind deeds are the fruits.
Take care of your garden, and keep out the weeds,
fill it with sunshine, kind words and kind deeds."
                                    —*Henry Wadsworth Longfellow*

Relationships, like gardens, need nourishment. In particular, there are four seeds that nourish the depth and quality of understanding and intimacy in all your relationships—deep listening, loving speech, gratitude and generosity. These represent the foundation of loving communication, the soil of our connection and the language of the heart. They are the means of expressing loving-kindness, compassion, joy and equanimity. Loving communication offers us an understanding of and desire to solve our conflicts and find peace within. As the basis of our daily interactions, it becomes the path that expedites our journey to wholeness.

Based on this understanding, you will develop skillful means of sharing gratitude and generosity. With every in-breath, we experience the beauty of life with gratitude. With every out-breath, we realize that we have enough and so we can demonstrate our love and compassion through generosity. These qualities illuminate an abundance of ways to "whisper" I love you!

CHAPTER 12

Deep Listening

*We have two ears and one mouth so that we can
listen twice as much as we speak."* —*Epictetus*

How many times are you with someone
yet not really there? How often have you
shared deeply with another but not felt
that you'd been heard? Our society is
plagued with parents who aren't present
for their children and co-workers more
interested in what is on their computer
screen or phone than the person visiting
their office. With the ability for 24/7 connectivity, we often get so busy tending
our social networks that we miss the
most precious connections that are right
in front of us—connections with ourselves and others. Thanks to technology,
people around the globe are more in

touch and yet simultaneously more isolated. The familiar habit energies of "hurry sickness," a need to judge or fix problems, or the
need to defend our view keeps us from being present with another.
In this chapter we will discover the practice of deep listening, both
to relieve another's suffering and to create understanding, which is
the nature of true love.

Deep listening encompasses more than just being attentive to what another is expressing. It has far-reaching implications for the depth at which we can be present with another. Also known as "compassionate listening," "generous listening," "listening below the noise" or "listening with the third ear," it implies that we are engaged in an open, non-judgmental way. We are not listening for a break in the conversation so that we may add our perspective or opinions. We are listening in a way that helps people better understand themselves by offering them the freedom to express themselves openly. Our focus is completely on them, and we need do nothing but sit in compassionate silence and give our attention. Perhaps this can best be described as listening from the heart.

Recall the Buddhist figure, Avalokiteshvara, or Kwan Yin, mentioned in Chapter 9. She represents the capacity each of us has to listen to suffering with compassion and presence. She reminds us that these qualities or seeds are within us. Looking back on my life, I am aware that the people who made the strongest impact were often those who were there for me unconditionally, listening with an open heart. They had no agenda other than to allow me to express my thoughts and feelings at the time—positive or negative. These individuals came in the form of therapists, family members and friends. Their generous listening was instrumental in relieving my suffering at the time. My greatest aspiration continues to be to keep my heart, mind and hands open to relieve suffering by simply listening deeply.

Communication Barriers

In her book *The Zen of Listening*, Rebecca Shafir suggests that we all have "communication walls" that limit our ability to listen. These barriers include the environment (such as background noise), racial background, age, appearance and status, all of which can create an imbalance before communication begins. Our own prejudices and biases can impact our ability to be with a person who appears to be different. Often our own agenda and desire for a specific outcome limit our ability to truly hear what is alive within another person. And one of the greatest barriers to being present is our own negative self-talk, which too often filters out the true message.

Children are wonderful examples of how to listen without barriers or biases. One of my favorite stories is of a young boy who would often visit an elderly neighbor whose wife had died. One day the boy's mother was surprised to learn the beloved neighbor had nominated her son for an award to be given by a local organization on compassion. The parents attended the ceremony and were pleased to see their son receive one of the awards. Upon returning home the mother said to the boy, "I am so proud of you! What did you say to our neighbor that was so helpful?" The young boy replied, "Oh mom, I didn't say much. All I did was listen to him cry."

Presence: Key to Deep Listening

Presence can be described as feeling that no one else is more important than the person you are with. It is the gift of undivided attention. Someone has truly shown up for you, and their body language and other behaviors demonstrate they are with you not only physically, but also in mind and spirit.

We know we are listening or listened to when there is an awareness demonstrated by body language, an understanding of the words, and a connection with the feelings conveyed as well as a deeper understanding of the values that are illuminated by sharing. The message we want to give with our bodies is I am here for you. Then our work is simply to listen to what is being said—the words—as well as what is not being said–the underlying feelings—that inspire intimacy and understanding. In my days as a university professor, my students would often stop by my office to hand in a paper or discuss a classroom issue. On many occasions, however, their body language belied a deeper reason for their visit. When appropriate, I would look into their eyes and ask, "How are you really doing?" Sometimes the visitor would cry. At other times he or she would sit down quietly, grateful to have an opportunity to share a personal story or dilemma. When I practiced deep listening, visitors often left the office feeling nurtured and—most importantly—heard. In seed language, they were given the opportunity to touch deeper seeds, such as anger and fear, which were then allowed to circulate between the mind and store consciousness. In those moments of congruence, they were free to be themselves.

Understanding: Focus of Deep Listening

The first goal in deep listening is to develop an understanding of the other. Our purpose in listening is not to win an argument or solve a problem. Often our own personal stories or mental formations can cloud our interactions. At times our stereotypes can create a limited view of the other and often negate the potential of creating emotional intimacy in the relationship. Personally, I find that I have the need to try to fix a problem being shared by making what I feel are helpful suggestions to the issue at hand. In so doing I often miss an opportunity to understand the other's journey, to see them reflected in the light of who they truly are as individuals, and to learn from their sharing.

Sometimes we find ourselves in the position of listening to someone in great pain or deep grief. They may rage at the unfairness of the situation or express profound sadness in their circumstances. At such times it is tempting to temper or discount their feelings to make ourselves feel more comfortable. However, the art of deep listening—together with the ability to maintain equanimity—can be the greatest gifts to another on their path to healing. Breathing deeply, listening with an open heart, and adopting a non-judgmental attitude are all part of watering the seeds of loving-kindness and compassion rather than fear and negativity.

"The first duty of love is to listen."   —Paul Tillich

Practice:

LISTEN TO YOURSELF

With mindfulness we are able to explore the pathways to the present moment. We recall that our body, our feelings, our perceptions, our mental formations, and consciousness are always offering us insights. If we can truly listen to ourselves, we create the perfect conditions for listening to others. What is my body saying? What am I feeling? How is this influencing my consciousness?

STOP

Stopping is the very important practice of staying in the present moment. It entails not being caught in the past or focusing on the future. You know you have stopped when you recognize and are totally focused on the person before you. One way to enhance the process is to remember to take several breaths and center yourself. You don't need to announce that you are stopping. Slowly begin to focus on the moment, and the other person will soon mirror your centeredness.

CALM YOURSELF TO QUIET YOUR MIND

Many spiritual practitioners say that the ability to calm the mind indicates one's growth on the spiritual path. In traditional meditation, the mind quiets when there is a focus on the breath or a mantra, such as "I am here for you." A mantra, as we have learned, is a phrase that, when repeated, supports the practice of being focused. It reinforces the desired behavior. When sitting next to another, allow them to become your focus and calming device—the person becomes the mantra, so to speak. The mind will then naturally quiet, especially when coordinated with our natural breath.

LOOK DEEPLY

Looking deeply is a more intense way of connecting with yourself and others. This harkens back to the concept of "Interbeing"—the state of peace and presence in which one can see the connection between others and oneself. In this state of awareness, we realize that we are not separate from one another. The feelings of another become our own, and we experience compassion. Mother Teresa said: "If we have no peace, it is because we have forgotten that we belong to each other." This connection is the deepest form of intimacy we can experience, and it creates the conditions for developing compassion.

LISTEN WITH COMPASSION
Our main purpose in listening is to relieve the suffering in others. Listening with compassion is one of the best ways to relieve suffering.

LISTEN WITHOUT JUDGMENT
Learn to listen without judgment, defensiveness, argument or interruption. If we can be patient and listen to another, they will feel heard, and much of their suffering will be mitigated. Nonjudgmental acceptance and faith in the other is key. If we have to defend ourselves, win, or exercise supremacy in any way, there is no space to hear the other.

Mantras:
- I am here for you.
- I listen deeply to understand.
- I listen to relieve your suffering.
- In this moment, you are the most important person in my life.

> *"I suspect that the most basic and powerful way to connect to another person is to listen. Just listen. Perhaps the most important thing we ever give each other is our attention. And especially if it's given from the heart. When people are talking, there's no need to do anything but receive them."* —Rachel Naomi Remen

CHAPTER 13

Loving Speech

"Words can travel thousands of miles. May my words create mutual understanding and love. May they be as beautiful as gems, as lovely as flowers." —*Thich Nhat Hanh*

Last month, I saw a parent angrily berate her child in a supermarket when he reached for one of the many colorful distractions children often face in such venues. I watched the child's face and saw his spirit diminish as seeds of fear, anger and frustration were watered before my eyes. Words have power. They can be used mindfully and responsibly to inspire, motivate, create, heal, and offer guidance and support. They can also hurt, abuse, divide, attack, lie, gossip, judge, and diminish.

Buddha once said, "A person is born with an axe in his mouth. He whose speech is unwholesome cuts himself with an axe." The blade wounds us, for what we say of others is often true of ourselves. Our communication often reflects the seeds within us that have been nurtured or neglected.

There is a tribe in East Africa that considers the day a child becomes a thought in its mother's mind to be the child's birth date. Aware of her intention to conceive a child, the mother then goes off to sit alone under a tree, where she sits and listens until she can hear the song of the child she hopes to conceive. After the birth, all the villagers learn the song of their new member and sing it to the child when it falls or hurts itself. It is sung in times of triumph, or in rituals and initiations. The song becomes a part of the marriage ceremony when the child is grown, and at the end of life, his or her loved ones will gather around the deathbed and sing this song for the last time. What an amazing way to communicate love to a child—or to anyone, for that matter. What would it be like if such consciousness was an integral part of our speech? How would those we love be different if the seed of loving speech became our song—ongoing messages given with attention, appreciation, and affection? I am reminded by a plaque on our wall, "My beloved knows my song and sings it to me when I forget."

Foundations for Loving Speech

In classic Buddhism, loving speech is called right speech and is part of what is known as the Eight Fold Path. In practicing right speech, one refrains from not telling the truth, exaggerating, forked tongue—that is, saying one thing to one person and another to someone else—and filthy language that insults or abuses another. The Bible reminds us "Thou shalt not bear false witness against thy neighbor," and the beautiful Quaker saying "Speak only if you can improve the silence" reminds us of the importance of choosing our words wisely.

Loving Speech Is Speaking from the Heart

Loving Speech implies deep listening, taking the time to be still and quiet long enough to listen to what takes place in our minds and hearts so that we are better equipped to respond mindfully to others. We usually tend to speak from the head rather than from the heart. It is typical to be thinking and planning what to say when others are still speaking—a hint that we are about to speak from the head. At other times, the need to be right interferes with heart communication. Do you want to be right, or do you want to be happy? Today, I am more interested in the communication that comes from the heart—focusing on feelings and happiness vs. righteousness or superiority. These are the cornerstones for emotional intimacy and a means of developing a deeper connection with others.

> *"No man should talk one way with his lips and think another way in his heart."* —*The Talmud*

Watering the Seed of Loving Speech

One helpful guideline to support loving speech is to reflect on what is called "The Fourth Mindfulness Training" created by Thich Nhat Hanh: "Knowing that words can create happiness or suffering, I am committed to speaking truthfully using words that inspire confidence, joy, and hope."

In every moment, as you are about to communicate electronically or verbally, mindfully stop and realize the potential impact of the message you are about to send. Does it inspire confidence, joy and hope? Or does it foster greater suffering in yourself and others? A friend who responds to your illness with "I send you healing light and energy," versus "Why haven't you taken better care of yourself?" is watering the seeds of loving-kindness in you with loving speech.

We can nurture this quality by being open to the ideas and stories of others. Everyone has a story to tell! Most people want to share their life's journey with others. An effective way to let the other person know you have heard them is to use reflective listening. This is a process of paraphrasing, in our own words, what was just ex-

125

pressed. It involves two key steps: seeking to understand the speaker's idea and then offering the idea back to the speaker to confirm that you heard correctly. For example, if someone shares a story of loss with you, you might respond with, "It sounds like your heart is hurting today." This practice means that we are engaging in two-way communication rather than a parallel conversation consisting of separate sound bites of each individual's thoughts.

The next phase of loving speech is to go beyond simply the words being shared to look deeply at the content. The work on Non-Violent Communication (NVC) by Marshall Rosenburg offers a wonderful guide for observing and listening to what influences our well-being. The NVC model suggests that there are feelings and needs in all types of communication. Simply said, when we feel energetic, joyous, fulfilled and inspired, our physical, emotional and spiritual needs are met. Conversely, when we are feeling angry, distressed, sad and irritated, our needs are not being met. By making a connection between feelings and needs, the depth of our communication will grow. For, by bearing this connection in mind on an ongoing basis, we get to the heart of what is being said, and compassion becomes our natural response.

Loving speech is best achieved by our awareness of how our words reduce suffering and inspire hope—or how they create more suffering. Knowing the power our words can have, it is important to consider the impact of what we say. How will our next words water the seeds of joy, compassion and equanimity? How do my words fuel the seeds of anger, fear or jealousy? When I am not calm and peaceful, my words will more likely be harsh and harmful. When I am mindful and notice that my speaking is a reflection of my thinking, I am able to stop and recognize my old habit energy. When I am peaceful and open, my words will invite openness and water the positive seeds in others.

Practice:

LISTEN WITH AN OPEN HEART AND MIND

Focusing on what the other is saying is more important than what we think we need to say. It honors them as a person and offers time to share their story. Deep listening always precedes loving speech.

CREATE SPACE WITHIN THE DIALOGUE

Pausing between comments with a conscious breath is a wonderful practice. The need to speak has conditioned us to respond robotically and hurriedly to what is said. With a pause and a breath, we may discover that what seemed urgent a moment ago is no longer as vital.

POSTPONE COMMUNICATION WHEN ANGRY

Typically, anger only escalates a conversation, especially if either party is defending their point of view and feels the need to be right. If the feelings are volatile, pause and come back to your breathing. Take another breath to further calm yourself and stop talking. Become aware of what you are feeling in that moment. If the anger is high, ask politely if this conversation could be continued when you are both calm and relaxed. Ideally, you both will be able to calm down and look deeply at the roots of this the anger and conflict. Continuing in this moment will create more hurt feelings and water the negative seeds.

CONSIDER THE FOLLOWING QUESTIONS WHEN SHARING

Dharma teacher, Gil Fronsdal, suggests we ask the following questions before speaking: Is it true? Is it kind? Is it useful? Is it timely? and Does it help us connect?

BE MINDFUL IN ELECTRONIC COMMUNICATION

Every day we receive literally hundreds of sound bytes of information, from a few words to elaborate electronic letters. Instant responses are the norm, but they can often be the source of suffering. Take a breath and be mindful as you reply, or maybe even hold your response for a day.

Mantras:

- I will not spread news that I do not know to be certain, and I will not criticize or condemn things of which I am not sure.
- I will speak from the heart when it is true and when it is appropriate.
- I vow to learn to speak truthfully, with words that inspire self-confidence, joy, and hope.

> *"Kind words can be short and easy to speak, but their echoes are truly endless."* —*Mother Teresa*

CHAPTER 14

Gratitude

"Thank you for everything. I have no complaints."
—words of a Buddhist nun

In the book *The Hiding Place* by Corrie ten Boom, the author recounts her experience in Ravensbruck concentration camp during World War II. She and her sister Betsy had been imprisoned there for having helped Dutch Jews escape the Nazis. Each evening, after a long, horrific day of forced labor, the sisters led a prayer group in the midst of the filth and horror of the camp. They closed each evening with a list of things for which they were grateful that day. One night Corrie was shocked to hear her sister say she was thankful for the fleas. "But Corrie, in the Bible it says we must give thanks for all things!" Later she learned that the only reason the vicious guards did not come into their bunk areas to harass and beat them was because they were afraid of the fleas!

Gratitude is both a state of mind and a way of life. It helps us to be present for all of life—especially our relationships. Qualities associated with gratitude include appreciation, thankfulness and generosity. Through the practice of gratitude we are enticed to become aware of the wonders of life and, as a result, find happiness in the present moment. Expressing gratitude requires true presence. Being aware of what we are grateful for is a "bell of mindfulness," an opportunity to "wake up" in our daily interactions. In this state of awareness we naturally look for the positive aspects of all our connections.

A species whose presence, absence, or relative well-being in a given environment is indicative of the health of its ecosystem as a whole is known as an "indicator species." Gratitude can be likened to that concept; when present, it offers an indication of the health and well-being of the person and their community. To be grateful is to be mindful—remembering to stop, calm, and look deeply long enough to recognize what is before us at any moment. With gratitude, the seeds of mindfulness, loving-kindness, joy and generosity are also nurtured because all the seeds in the garden of our consciousness are interrelated. For example, when the seed of loving speech is practiced, gratitude is often expressed as well. When the seed of deep listening is practiced, the seed of compassion can also be watered. In essence, all the seeds of our consciousness "inter-are."

Generating Gratitude

To generate gratitude, we start by acknowledging that our lives are made possible by the lives of many who sacrificed so we could be here today. To notice the tender smile or the spacious presence of a friend requires us to connect within their heart space, which in turn requires by being present long enough to receive these gifts. To be grateful for the food that we eat, we must become aware of the many hands that created it, as well as the sun, the rain and other environmental variables. This means looking deeply at the origin of this gift of nourishment. How many hands made it possible to be where we are today? How many shoulders are we standing on?

How many people watered seeds within us to help make us what we are today?

> *"Let us be grateful to the people who make us happy; they are the charming gardeners who make our souls blossom."*
> —Marcel Proust

As Benedictine monk Brother David-Steindl Rast, one of the leading proponents of gratitude as a spiritual practice, explains, "As I express my gratitude, I become more deeply aware of it. And the greater my awareness, the greater my need to express it." He clearly suggests that the more we practice watering this seed, the more sustained and grateful we become.

Gratitude is also inspired by the impermanence of life. Mortality is part of the human condition. We all get sick, grow old, and die. Since there is no escape from this reality, it serves us to direct our attention to the gifts of our lives and water the seeds they engender. Often, for example, it is the death of a loved one that reminds us of the preciousness of life, the importance of living in the now, and the need to be grateful for our blessings. This is it! This is the time to be grateful for who we are and what we have, and to live in such a way that our legacy will be one of loving-kindness.

True gratitude also calls us to be grateful for all of our opportunities, even those that may have been painful or unpleasant. Those are often the places we find we have learned the most about ourselves, our strength, our stamina, and our courage. Most everyone is grateful when things are going well. The challenge is to find the gifts, the wisdom, and the grace in our most difficult life experiences.

Several years ago I had the privilege of traveling with Thich Nhat Hanh and a Western delegation to visit Buddhist temples in China. It was a remarkable experience to return to the source of Chan practice (original Zen) and visit temples where the practice of Zen originated. Typically we would visit each temple and reside there for three or four days to experience these beautiful root practices and the teachings. However, from a Western perspective, there were times when our living conditions could be considered quite challenging. After a few days, Thich Nhat Hanh was made aware of the complaints, and during one of his dharma talks noted the concern by saying, "If you are not grateful, you are suffering." Ever since that trip, I have used this statement as a mantra and way of changing the music when my focus is on the suffering.

So often, preoccupied with things we cannot change, we lose opportunities to focus on the gifts that are available to us. In his book *Beauty*, author and poet John O'Donohue maintains that when we're in this mindset we miss the "luminous moments of our life" and he urges us to focus on the beauty that life continually offers us—the emergence of a full moon after days of cloudy skies, the smile on a loved one's face, the dew on the morning grass, the music of laughter, the feel of the sun on our body. By simply placing our attention on what is beautiful, it is easy to selectively water the seed of gratitude everywhere we turn.

> *"In difficult times you should always carry something beautiful in your mind."* —Blaise Pascal

In developing the seed of gratitude, it is essential to be mindful. Taking time to appreciate each breath—each moment—waters the seeds of mindfulness and gratitude. Unless I am present for life, it will pass me by while I go about my business. True gratitude loves what is and is able to say, "Thank you, I have no complaints."

> *Breathing in, I am grateful for this moment.*
> *Breathing out, I smile.*

Practice:

SEED AUDIT

How fortunate we are to be alive! Rather than focus on what is not going well, take time daily to reflect on all the people who made your life possible. Whose shoulders are you standing on? What seeds were watered to bring you to this place in your life? Who were the major gardeners? Have you shared your gratitude with these people lately? Now is the time—if not now, when? When you are ready, include gratitude for the people who have watered negative seeds. How have they helped you to grow and change?

GRATITUDE KEEPS US CURRENT

When we are truly mindful, we can't help being grateful. At the end of the day, reflect on what you have been grateful for to keep the seed of gratitude alive in your mind consciousness longer and so develop deep roots in your store consciousness.

COUNT YOUR BLESSINGS

In the Jewish tradition, during the time of King David a plague took the lives of nearly 100 people each day. As a means of prayer and gratitude, the sages suggested that people look at their blessings and reflect on 100 of them each day. This is a great practice for the present time. At the end of each day, sit quietly and recall the blessings of that day. At first this may be challenging because most of us do not pause long enough to look deeply at the myriad of little blessings that have made our day. Using this practice at the end of the day prepares our hearts to look for blessings when we begin the next day. In seed language, this is considered "deep watering."

Other practices to water the seed of gratitude include:
- Saying a prayer before a meal—How many hands made this possible?
- Writing a note to someone who touched your life in the distant or recent past.
- Taking a slow mindful walk and thinking of people you are grateful for. Silently, with each step, breathe and be grateful for each person.

Mantras:

- I am happy and grateful for... (fill in the blank and repeat as often as possible).
- Big or small, positive or negative, I appreciate it all.
- I am grateful for your presence in my life.
- I am grateful for my/your well-being.

"You say grace before meals. All right. But I say grace before the concert and the opera, and grace before the play and pantomime, and grace before I open a book, and grace before sketching, painting, and swimming, fencing, boxing, walking, playing, dancing, and grace before I dip the pen in ink." —G. K. Chesterton

CHAPTER 15

Generosity

"Gardeners are known for their generous natures. If we are skilled, our gardens are always overflowing." —Geri Larkin

Generosity is a central tenant in all major religions and philosophies. Jose Hobday, a Native American elder and storyteller, explains in *Simple Living*, "We used to say you could tell if a person was an authentic native by whether or not she had a red heart. A red heart had to do with whether the heart had blood from being massaged by good works, especially sharing." Catholic contemplative Henri Nouwen, in his book *Sabbatical Journey*, says, "I think that generosity has many levels. We have to think generously, speak generously, and act generously. Thinking well of others and speaking well of others is the basis for generous giving. Generosity cannot come from guilt or pity. It has to come from hearts

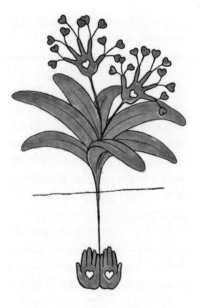

that are fearless and free and are willing to share abundantly all that is given to us."

In order to come to that deep place in our hearts, generosity needs to blossom from our ability to see the Interbeing nature between us and the receiver. It is like the right hand does not need to thank the left hand for cutting the food. When walls of separation are broken down, we are in flow and giving from one heart to another. There is no tally going on inside our minds. When the walls of us vs. them have been broken down, it is so natural to give to another. To give knowing that we have enough allows us to have no attachment to getting something in return.

Charity or Generosity?

The words charity and generosity are often used synonymously. However, Lucinda Vardy and John Costa in *Being Generous* delineate between the two words by sharing that "Charity is being moved to give. Generosity is being moved to change. With charity, the transaction is giver to receiver. The relationships in generosity are interactive and more mutually expansive. Charity is most often a reaction or responsibility based on sympathy, while generosity is also an anticipation or imagination sparked by empathy."

Several years ago on a pilgrimage to India my student companions and I encountered endless rows of children lining the path to a sacred site where the Buddha spent five years in solitude and deprivation. These children were chanting "rupees, rupees" as they begged for money with open hands and sad faces. At first we offered some spare change; later we shared our food. But as the number children grew larger around every corner, it became impossible to continue to give what little we had. Our guide, Shantum Seth, also a Buddhist teacher, instructed us to bow while looking at the children with an open heart and not to look away. When we could no longer offer rupees or supplies, we could still offer a compassionate presence and generous heart.

A month after returning from our trip, the group explored the gifts that we gained from the India experience and how we might use them to water the seeds of gratitude and generosity in ourselves and the Indian people. The students went beyond charity as they expanded their view on how best to provide for those children in India, creating a project to support a school for untouchable children in the city of Bodh Gaya. The project, called "Meditate/Educate," involved purchasing meditation cushion covers handmade by a poor tailor in that city. The purchase of the covers helped support the tailor's family, and the sale of the covers in the United States provided funds to support the education of one child per year at the school.

This one profound experience of charity expanded the students' empathy, which continues to overflow in their lives long after graduation. Many went on to careers in human services, including tours of duty in the Peace Corps. Keeping our hearts open to the suffering we encountered in the children moved us all to generate more good works and changed us all in profound ways. At a deep level we all seemed to feel that travelling to India for an educational experience was just a beginning. We felt called to respond to the disparity we witnessed between what we observed and what we ourselves experience in terms of material goods, health care and education. The seed of compassion was deeply watered and we felt moved to a more generous response.

Watering the Seed of Generosity

My friend Randall is a typical generous spirit. He is a veteran who lives alone in a small studio and gets along on a medical pension. A permanent back injury keeps him in bed much of the time. With no car and only enough worldly goods to fit into two suitcases, his simple lifestyle allows him to provide monthly donations to struggling charities and to do volunteer administrative work for various groups by using his laptop from bed. He truly represents the spirit of generosity in his willingness to support and serve others in a mindful way,

The benefits of Randall's simple and generous lifestyle were not apparent to him at first. Chronic illness and "problems of success" in his mid-adult life had him casting about for answers to his suffering. Then a fortuitous meeting with spiritual leaders who were aiding exiled Chinese students and Tibetans in California during the 90s revealed a simple solution to Randall's challenges. The core of that solution is well understood by most spiritual practices through the concept that the best and truest way to end one's own suffering is to help end that of another.

Generous people give unprompted by guilt, social pressure or to obtain a tax credit at the end of the year. Their generosity removes boundaries between themselves and others. As a result they feel more connected and experience "Interbeing." They give because after looking deeply at the suffering of a neighbor, family member or a stranger, they recognize their own suffering in the suffering of the other. In giving there is no separation. If, just for a moment, we stop and calm ourselves and look deeply at a homeless person and in that instant connect with an open heart, in that moment we have a choice to give or not. The giving is based on looking deeply to ascertain how best to support this stranger. In giving we actively demonstrate watering the seeds of loving-kindness, compassion, joy and equanimity.

Generosity is also a process of letting go. When I give something away it is no longer mine. This is seen developmentally, as a child struggles to share a toy and shouts "Mine!" This same attachment to things changes once we understand that objects no longer define us and may actually confine us. Many of us have "too many cows." This expression comes from a story during the time of the Buddha, when he encountered a man who was in great distress looking for his lost cows. "Have you seen my cows?" After leaving the scene, the Buddha shared, "We are lucky we don't have to worry about too many cows." Generosity becomes easier as we recognize that true happiness and freedom come from knowing we have enough and ultimately we are enough.

Jack Kornfield, in *A Path With Heart: a Guide Through the Perils and Promises of Spiritual Life* suggests that there are three levels of giving—tentative giving, brotherly or sisterly giving, and royal giving. These levels provide a template for helping us understand where we are in the process of learning to give and be generous. Think of the last time you gave something away. What were you thinking and feeling? Tentative giving usually comes with some form of hesitation, a desire to hold on a little more tightly to something rather than let it go. Brotherly or sisterly giving implies that there is an equal sharing of whatever it is that is needed. We are each invited to the table to share in the bounty or abundance. Royal givers give freely, no doubts, no hesitations. They give with only the well-being and happiness of others in mind.

Simply put, we give because we have been given to. All the gardeners who made it possible for us to be here today have offered us opportunities to practice gratitude and generosity. Like all the seeds, we "inter-are." We are not separate. Just as a gardener waters the garden, every plant and weed receives that which sustains life. We are then nourished by the harvest. When we nurture another's well-being and support them by watering the best seeds within, our relationship is also sustained, now and in the future.

> *Breathing in, I am grateful.*
> *Breathing out, I am generous.*

Practice:

DEVELOP A GENEROUS ATTITUDE TOWARD EVERYTHING

When you feel the desire to give, act on that desire. Water this seed when the heart calls. Doing so makes the most of the opportunity for the root of generosity to grow deep in our store consciousness. Mother Teresa reminds us, "We can do no great things, only small things with great love."

BE GENEROUS TO YOURSELF
It is important to nourish our inner garden first so that we can water the seeds in another. Taking time every day to stop, to find space and enjoy silence renews our ability to continue our generosity for others.

RECOGNIZE YOUR GIFTS...AND THEN GIVE THEM AWAY
We all have something unique to share with the world. The gifts you offer the world become your legacy and your continuation. Most people are remembered because of their generous spirit rather than their possessions.

PAY IT FORWARD
In this famous film, a young boy is motivated to create a school project in which he is encouraged to "think of a way to change our world, and put it into action." He takes three actions that make a difference in the lives of others and asks each of those people to do the same for three other people. His good deeds influenced others exponentially. This true story not only became a movie but also a movement to inspire others to water the seed of generosity. It invites us, when grateful, to say thank you and "pay it forward." It is a wonderful example of how generosity is generative and can be life-changing and transformational.

Mantras:
- Today, I am generous to myself in every way.
- I give my gifts freely and without any expectations.
- I let go of my attachments, I am free.

PART 5

Compost

"The organic gardener does not think of throwing away the garbage. She knows that she needs the garbage. She is capable of transforming the garbage into compost, so that the compost can turn into lettuce, cucumbers, radishes, and flowers again."
—Thich Nhat Hanh

As conscientious gardeners, we know we can create compost from decaying organic material, including leaves, manure and even the vegetable scraps from daily meals. When combined with the soil of our gardens, these "leftovers" offer the proper nutrients and texture to enable the garden to flourish and thrive. Without the compost, we would not benefit from the beauty and richness the garden can offer to body, mind, and spirit.

As caretakers of our spiritual and emotional gardens, we all have qualities or seeds within us that serve as compost in our daily lives. Like the leftovers that make up the compost that enriches our gardens, these seeds—fear, anger, doubt and jealousy—are not what spring to mind when we think of qualities we want to cultivate. But through the practice of mindfulness, we can stop and look deeply at these seeds to discover, understand and appreciate their value and importance in the garden of our consciousness.

Despite the plethora of compost seeds available to us for thorough exploration, anger, fear, doubt and jealousy seem most the relevant to examining our relationships. These seeds often have the deepest roots. As we unearth them, we will learn to transform these seeds of suffering into the compost necessary for love to blossom and flourish in ourselves and those we love.

As in our backyard gardens, weeds may not immediately offer the nutrients desired in our garden. Some weeds need to be rooted and the entire plant may need to be extricated from the garden. In some circumstances, some relationships do not work, and in order to protect the garden, a separation or boundary is necessary.

My mother was quite meticulous about de-rooting a dandelion, especially before it continued to flower into the puffy white seeds that caused more suffering for her. When the weed is seeding, it will create more weeds if allowed onto the compost pile. This same kind of sensitivity is necessary when the seeds of fear, anger, doubt and jealousy are surfacing in rage—they may create more damage to the relationship as a weed, and may not always be ripe for compost or positive growth.

> *"With the energy of mindfulness, you can look into the garbage and say: I am not afraid. I am capable of transforming the garbage back into love."* —Thich Nhat Hanh

CHAPTER 16

Fear

"Our deepest fears are like dragons guarding our deepest treasures."
—*Rainer Maria Rilke*

Several years ago, a student in one of my university classes shared with me that his father was dying of cancer. The thought of his father's death filled him with debilitating fear. Since his family lived nearby on the Oregon coast, we would often talk about life on the beach, which gave me an opportunity to help him examine one of our greatest fears–death. I asked him to reflect on the life of a wave as it parallels our own life. Every wave has a beginning, middle and end. When we no longer see the wave, has the wave died? Where did the wave go? As he thought about the tides, he realized that while his father would no longer be physically present in his life, he would continue in a new way.

As the disease progressed, the young man would talk with his father about the waves. Above his bed was a picture of an ocean scene, a daily reminder that, like a wave, we all come to an end, and yet we are never gone. During his final days their relationship deepened, and together they helped each other cope with their greatest fear.

"Let us look deeply at a wave in the ocean. It lives its life of a wave, but it lives the life of water at the same time. If the wave were able to turn toward itself and touch its substance, which is water, then it would be able to attain non-fear." —Thich Nhat Hanh

What Is Fear?

Fear is a powerful and unpleasant feeling of risk or danger, real or perceived. Common fears include public speaking, heights, intimacy, failure, death, rejection, being wrong, embarrassment, loss and loneliness—not to exclude phobias about snakes, spiders, dogs, change and the unknown. Fear can serve a purpose in our lives. It can heighten our awareness and prepare us to take action when a real problem arises. Healthy fear can save our life, as our limbic system is hard-wired to feed, flee and fight. When a driver cuts us off or we become embarrassed in front of our colleagues, our body instantly releases adrenalin to help us deal with the threat, imagined or real. Fear creates a state of alertness that helps us find the solutions we need for survival even faster than we can think what to do. This emotional intelligence offers us both life-saving actions and insights or intuition about what is happening. Mindfulness, meditation and prayer help calm these centers in our bodies.

The qualities and derivations of fear relate to the potential threat of what we feared. Anxiety is characterized by the anticipation of being harmed in the future, while fear is characterized by the anticipation of being harmed in the present. These states tend to merge into an overall feeling of distress and uncertainty in everyday life.

Unhealthy fears are often at the root of daily angst and distress. They keep us awake at night and often cause unhappiness. Unhealthy fear takes a toll on our lives. Consider a person who experiences the loss of a relationship. Typically, the individual shuts down and temporarily decides never to get involved again—the pain is too great and the cost too high. They may live in greater isolation because they fear further failure and rejection. They may think that they are unlovable, or fear that no one will ever be attracted to them again. Although these feelings are often part of a natural grief response, if they not are faced, experienced and transformed, they become our unfinished business which, when accumulated, keeps us from living our lives fully. Think how many hours we spend living in fear, stress, and mindlessness, losing precious time and energy that could be spent in happiness and love.

Most of our fears and worries are irrational and based on distorted thinking. Prolonged focus on the seed of fear influences our perceptions, and quickly becomes a mental formation or story. Its repetition in our mind allows it to take deep root in our store consciousness.

My favorite acronym to help understand fear is:

False
Evidence
Appearing
Real

Apply this acronym to a situation you currently fear. How much of what you fear is real, irrational, distorted?

Fear is like an onion with many layers and a core—peeling each layer may even bring tears. To explore the layers, I recall stories that friends have shared with me while experiencing a life-threatening illness. They report living in a state of shock followed by fear and anxiety. Even treatment for the illness causes fear to arise—"Will the treatment work? How will I know? Am I doing the right thing?" At some point the fear of death usually gets their full attention for the first time in their life. This overall reaction is a normal and healthy response to such pain and illness and, if used in positive ways, can be an invitation to feel more alive than ever before.

On the other hand, if a person resists their fear, that seed will be buried even deeper in the garden of their store consciousness. Denial and busyness are the most common outlets for those who refuse to stop and look deeply at fear, which could allow them to truly begin to understand the origin of the emotion and discover new ways to be with this powerful feeling.

Using mindfulness to look deeply at their fears, some have found themselves living with more joy, gratitude and appreciation, especially for the many small things they previously took for granted. For some, it prompted a personal inventory of what was unfinished in their life so that they could live in a deeper way by sharing, as Ira Byock says in his book, *The Four Things that Matter Most*: "Please forgive me. I forgive you. Thank you. I love you." Whenever we look at fear this way, we are looking beneath the layers to find the deeper issue around it—whether a loss of control or fear of being alone. The feeling may even go deeper to a fear of death, which often connects with the deeper "business" of our lives. Finally, as another friend once said, when fear arises now, I am able to avoid the consequences by being totally present in meditation and life in general.

Being with Fear

Being with fear means allowing ourselves to feel it rather than resist it when it arises. The key to managing fear and other challenging feelings is being aware of what is happening at a deeper level when fear comes to visit. *In Path with Heart,: a Guide Through the Perils and Promises of a Spiritual Life*, Jack Kornfield shares, "In ancient cultures shamans learned that to name that which they feared was a practical way to begin to have power over it. We have words and rituals for many of our great outer events, birth and death, war and peace, marriage, adventure, illness, but often we are ignorant of the names of the inner forces that move so powerfully through our hearts and lives." Few people are truly aware of their inner journey and the need to "name the demons" we encounter there, as well as those we meet in our outer journeys.

Naming our fear and looking for the deeper message behind that fear can often be healing. You might try having a conversation with the emotion. "Hello, Fear. What are you trying to tell me today?" Ask yourself, how intense is this feeling? What is my body telling me about this feeling? What are my perceptions? Are they true? Am I sure? What kind of story am I weaving around these feelings, and how is that story being planted and watered in my consciousness? Is this a familiar feeling to me? Am I "rubber banding" back to an earlier event that precipitated this same feeling? How am I experiencing fear in my body as it arises?

Whenever I experience a stronger than normal reaction to any event in my life, I discover that the compost seeds of fear, anger, inadequacy and jealousy have not been tossed, turned and transformed. The longer the rumination, the stronger that seed will become and the deeper it will be planted in the garden of our consciousness. A few practices will help you dig deep and allow the seeds of compost do their work in enriching your life.

Practice:

HAVE TEA WITH MARA

Ananda was the Buddha's main attendant and a very diligent student. One day Ananda sensed the presence of Mara, which represents our demons, and he asked the Buddha, "What should we do? Mara is here." The Buddha said, "Don't worry, Ananda. I will invite him for tea." Symbolically, Mara represents our suffering and is often fear based. In essence the Buddha said to make friends with fear rather than push it away. We can practice this quietly in meditation and by watering the seeds of deep listening and loving speech.

ALLOW FEAR TO TEACH

Fear can be a "bell of mindfulness" and a call to action. Fear can also be our teacher. As I grow older, I am more aware of fear as it relates to loss—identity, health, and even death. In exploring these fears I recall the words of Rabbi Hillel, "If not now, when?" and use fear as a reminder to complete any unfinished business so I can live fully.

REPLACE FEAR WITH LOVE

Fundamentally we could say there are only two feelings—love and fear. When we place too much attention on what we fear, we become more fearful. As you move through your day, note what has your attention. Author Gerald Jampolsky says, "Love is letting go of fear." We can practice this idea, learning to touch fear, experience fear, and then move our attention and intention back into a natural state of love.

PRACTICE METTA

One of the best antidotes to fear is metta practice. Instead of worrying about our fears and worries, we come back to basic loving-kindness practice.:

> *May I (you, we) be filled with loving-kindness.*
> *May I (you, we) be free of suffering.*
> *May I (you, we) find joy.*
> *May I (you, we) be well.*
> *May I (you, we) find peace.*

Mantra Practice:
- Today I aspire to look deeply at the cause of my fear.
- When fear arises, I consciously shift to loving others and myself.
- Fear is my teacher. Thank you for reminding me to focus on what I can control today and live my life in deeper ways.

CHAPTER 17

Anger

"It's not healthy to keep your anger inside for long. I always advise my friends, 'Do not keep your anger to yourself for more than one day.'" —*Thich Nhat Hanh*

You may recall my story about prison inmate JR. Since he is familiar with the concepts outlined in this book, I recently asked him to comment on the seeds that were watered in his life before he was incarcerated. "Looking back," he wrote, "I can now see that many seeds were randomly watered in my early life, predominantly the seeds of fear, anger and self-loathing. It seems like I watered these seeds more than any of the others." JR also interviewed other inmates and discovered that they too could relate to the extensive watering of negative seeds. One inmate reflected, "It was all about money as I was growing up, and so seeds of anger and greed grew especially fast in me." As JR lamented, "Had I watered the seeds of loving-kindness and compassion in myself, or had they been watered in me by others, I

would have been more loving and peaceful in my interactions with others. I most likely would not be here today."

The Roots of Our Anger

We all have our own messages about the seed of anger. For some, the expression of anger is frowned upon or even punished. My mother's response to me whenever she sensed I was angry was to say, "Gerald, be nice." For others, anger can be seen as a healthy means of eliminating stress or venting feelings of pain or grief. It's safe to say that we do not have many healthy models for the expression of anger in our society. Thus, this seed is often buried deep in the soil of our consciousness.

Like a garden, our consciousness is vulnerable to a wide range of conditions. Some individuals grew up on a steady diet of anger within their families of origin or in their past and current relationships. We have all experienced a deluge of anger in the forms of media violence and displays of cruelty and hostility. Younger generations have stored such images via video games and television that may continually water the seed of anger. The expansion of technology coupled with new forms of entertainment—seduced and driven by profitability—offer future challenges for parents and society as a whole.

"I don't get angry, I get ulcers instead." —Woody Allen

Research suggests that anger lasting longer than twenty seconds is usually connected to something other than the recent trigger for that anger, typically some unfinished business or something "stuffed" from the past. Years ago, I was jogging and a driver nearly ran me off the road. I just missed ending up on the hood of his car. In a rage, my heart racing, I pounded my fists on the hood of his car before running away from the experience. My anger in that moment was obviously directed at the driver, but much later I discovered my anger had more to do with the pain and grief of a difficult relationship I was in at the time. When you can make a healthy connection between what is happening in the moment and what has happened in past, you create the ideal condition for understanding the anger and transforming the seed through mindful awareness. This awareness creates a connection and a circulation between anger in the mind consciousness and anger in the store consciousness—the beginning step for transformation.

Impact of Anger

Most of the stress we experience can be connected to negative feelings, such as anger and fear. Anger activates our nervous system in the same way that fear excites our limbic system to initiate the fight or flight response. If we keep unhealthy anger alive, it keeps the sympathetic nervous system simmering even during times of rest, and thus the body is fully activated during states of anger and fear.

Some individuals walk around with what is called "free floating hostility." The seed of anger is just below the surface of the soil, ready to explode at the slightest provocation. You can often discern your own level of equanimity and mindfulness practice when you are confronted with challenging situations. For example, how do you respond when driving in heavy traffic and someone cuts you off? Are you able to witness the provocation, or do you immediately explode or feel compelled to gesture angrily or rage back? Does this experience remind you of other frustrating experiences and thus add to your already smoldering feelings? Are you reflecting on the situation mindfully? Are you able to determine how much of your feelings are connected to the experience at hand or whether they have their roots in past events?

"For every minute you are angry, you lose sixty seconds of happiness."
—Ralph Waldo Emerson

Mindfulness and Anger

In the garden of our consciousness, we have the seeds of suffering and the seeds of love. Anger represents a negative energy and is a primary compost seed indicative of pain and suffering. Anger rarely exists in a vacuum. It is nearly always connected to emotions such as fear, hurt, betrayal as well as the images and stories about anger we carry within our consciousness. As in any garden, the flowers and weeds intertwine and synergistically survive off the energy of each other.

The seed or practice of mindfulness is the best antidote to anger. We have learned that by stopping and calming ourselves we are present to feel the feeling. By breathing and looking deeply with the eyes of mindfulness, we are able to experience the anger within our body, recognize the feeling, explore the perceptions (true or false), and realize that anger is a mental formation or story we are creating. The longer we hold the seed of anger above ground in our mind consciousness, the deeper its roots will be in the future. Like a dandelion, it will continue to return until the root is weeded out of the soil.

When the seed of anger emerges in our mind consciousness, we can use our tool of mindfulness to work with it. We can breathe, stop, calm and look deeply at this anger rather than push it deeper and deeper within. We can then ask ourselves, "What is this anger? What is it really about? How can I explore this opportunity to learn something about this feeling and myself." Dig deep to find the very root.

Transforming the Seed of Anger

We can think of transforming this seed by reflecting on a parent's response to a crying baby. As the mother or father hears their child cry, they are alerted that something is wrong, the baby is calling for help. Anger offers the same kind of message. As a parent picks up the crying baby, he or she holds the infant and searches for what might be wrong. Is the baby hungry, or does she need her diaper changed? A parent will hold the child close, calm her, and look for what needs to be done to relieve the child's suffering.

We can respond to and transform anger in much the same way. As anger arises and emerges in our consciousness, we can recognize it, and rather than ignore or deny it, we can mindfully embrace the emotion. Breathing in, I am aware of my anger. Breathing out, I embrace my anger. With one in-breath and out-breath, relief is on the way. During these moments of mindfulness, summon feelings of loving-kindness, compassion and equanimity so that in those moments you are free to examine the true source of the anger and release it.

An interesting way of connecting with the seed of anger is to imagine what you look like when you are angry. What did I look like when I was slamming my fist on the hood of that car years ago? The act of stepping back and witnessing ourselves during a moment of anger can be both enlightening and humbling. Who is this raging person? Where did his/her anger come from?

Practice:

PAY ATTENTION

Learn to listen to anger and how it influences your body, feelings, perceptions, mental formations and consciousness. How is anger serving you and how are you serving others who are angry? As good gardeners, we must realize that punishing another will not solve the problem but will simply escalate the feelings of anger. John Gottman, psychologist and author of *The Seven Principles of Making Marriage Work*, writes that it is important to avoid "harsh start ups" in our interactions. Harsh start-ups are often generated by anger, and they are a slippery slope leading downward into great anguish and potentially greater anger and confusion. It is never wise to begin communication—especially to solve a problem or address a conflict—when one or both partners are angry. Learning to mindfully soften our communication start-ups, especially after someone has been angry, will offer us a greater opportunity to resolve the difficulty. Put aside any thought of criticizing the other or recalling things that have been stored up for years. Instead, water the positive seeds in that individual as a starter, and the chance for creating reconciliation and understanding will be much greater.

Anger as a Gift

Many people believe that when we are angry, we need to vent and give anger free reign. I recall workshops in which people would throw dishes, pound on pillows and try to tear phone books to discharge the anger. While this may provide immediate relief, we could take the perspective that these forms of release could actually be considered practicing anger! The physical qualities of the anger may be released, but in fact the root of the anger may grow stronger.

Instead, we can choose to bring ourselves into a mindful state, perhaps by taking a mindful walk, and explore our anger by looking for what it can teach us about ourselves and our relationships with others. In this way, our anger becomes a guide or even a gift to deeper awareness and growth. Rather than use our anger to attack, to wound, to accuse, or to hurt another, we can say, "This anger stops with me. I will mindfully explore this seed in me and transform it into something meaningful and healing."

> *"The demons in our lives are the bearers of gifts hidden under their wings."* —Sarah Ban Breathnacht

Guided Meditations

As we have practiced before, guided meditations always involve the breath and a means of stopping and calming ourselves. This centering is necessary before we can look deeply at the source of our anger. You may find it helpful to create a personal guided meditation to help you explore anger in your life.

Examples:

Breathing in, I am aware of the anger within me (or other person).
Breathing out, I am aware of the suffering that this anger may cause.
Breathing in, I am aware of the anger in myself.
Breathing out, I look for the cause of that anger.

Mantras:

- I acknowledge the anger within me and the suffering it causes me and those around me.
- I look deeply at the seed of anger within me and trace its root to its origin in my past.
- I mindfully approach my loved one with loving-kindness as we seek to resolve disagreement.
- I embrace anger as a teacher so I may experience that feeling and release it from my mind consciousness.

CHAPTER 18

Jealousy

"Our jealous worries are the poisonous weeds of life's garden and should be rooted out instantly." — *George Wharton James*

Perhaps no other story so dramatically exemplifies the seed of jealousy as the Biblical tale of brothers Cain and Abel. Cain, a farmer, and Abel, a shepherd, shared a perfect life together. When God preferred Abel's offering of a first-born lamb to Cain's offering of grain, Cain's jealousy burned until it became hatred, and he killed his brother, Abel. While Cain was sick with regret over his hostile action, the damage was done. What damage has the seed of jealousy created in your life and your relationships? Can you recognize the seed of jealousy buried deep within your store consciousness?

Faces of Jealousy

When we ponder the seed of jealousy, we discover the desire to have something we do not have, or the fear that what we do have will be taken from us. Look under the umbrella of jealousy and you will find envy, covetousness, resentment, possessiveness, bitterness and spite. Jealousy is often a favorite topic of newspaper advice columns or television and radio talk shows, and it's no surprise that jealousy is one of the most common sources of irritation for couples seeking marriage counseling.

Jealousy also exposes our ego, which is often fueled by feelings of lack, inadequacy and competition. Someone else's accomplishments, joy, or possessions somehow undermines or belittles your own. If someone gets a promotion, it means you won't. If someone is accomplished, it means you may have to work even harder to be noticed. The dance becomes one of ego vs. others. You diminish yourself and your accomplishments when you envy another or covet what they have. David Richo, in *How To Be an Adult in Relationships*, shares that "Ego-driven jealousy exposes our possessiveness, our dependency, our resentment of another's freedom, our refusal to be vulnerable."

Impact of Jealousy

The seed of jealousy, more than any other, puts us face-to-face with our attachments as we turn our attention to all that we are "missing" in life, and respond or react to them with discontentment and resentment. At the very core of the seed of jealousy lies the profound sense that we lack value, and thus we find ourselves looking outside ourselves to either prove we are enough or, sadly, to acquire things that bring us a sense of worth. Personally, for example, I touch the seed of jealousy when a friend announces an upcoming trip to Hawaii in the winter months when my home state of Oregon is drenched with rain, or perhaps when I hear someone present a talk more eloquently than I do. The thief of comparison always robs me of the opportunity to appreciate my own unique gifts as well as those of others.

Like other compost seeds, jealousy is an indicator species, requiring us to look deeply and discover why this story or mental formation has been created—and what other seeds or qualities are connected to it. As we have learned, we should not resist the emotions brought to the surface by compost seeds, but embrace them as teachers and opportunities for growth.

In recognizing the feeling of jealousy, be aware of its influence on your body. What happens when you perceive that something will be taken from you? Notice how your body contracts, tenses and literally moves into a protective state. Recognize how the feelings of fear and anger often partner with jealousy and add to the deluge of emotional arousal you experience. Be aware of how, in moments of jealousy, you can easily forget to listen deeply and use loving speech, and may thus speak mindlessly and regrettably. Pay attention to how, as a result of dwelling on this story or mental formation, you experience more self-doubt. The longer these thoughts, feelings and perceptions are watered, the deeper the roots grow into our store consciousness.

Being With Jealousy

"Every mental formation—anger, jealousy, and despair—is sensitive to mindfulness the way all vegetation is sensitive to sunshine. By cultivating the energy of mindfulness, you can heal your body and your consciousness." —Thich Nhat Hanh

Jealousy can be taken as a wonderful opportunity to shine the light of mindfulness on the seed before it takes over your entire garden. In the moment you notice a spark of jealousy arising, come back to your breath. Breathing is the key to stabilizing the feeling so that it does not proliferate through our perceptions and the mental formations or stories we create. With jealousy, as with other challenging seeds, the first step is to become aware without judgment or criticism. Using mindfulness together with deep listening and loving speech, we can begin to see our Interbeing nature with others, where competition and envy become unnecessary because, in essence, we are all connected. Another's joy, success, or accomplishments become our own.

Most of our suffering comes from a lack of equanimity—from a state of feeling inferior. This label simply separates us from others. When we can truly see each person as our brother and our sister, we discover that true happiness comes through our Interbeing nature— we are all connected so there is no need to dwell in jealousy.

Thich Nhat Hanh gives the example of a person who always walks mindfully within their community. Instead of being jealous of that person, we could admire his or her diligence and mindfulness, aspiring to cultivate those qualities in ourselves. Equanimity enables us to appreciate and love those around us.

Although you typically take sides in your mind, strive to treat everyone as an equal. As Thich Nhat Hanh has said, "It is the kind of love that a mother has for all of her children even though one is easier to love than another, some bring suffering into her life, and others make her feel sad." By practicing equanimity, all are seen as equal and so everyone has a refuge or haven when emotional waters are rough. Equanimity is one of the best antidotes to jealousy.

> *"Instead of comparing our lot with that of those who are more fortunate than we are, we should compare it with the lot of the great majority of our fellow men. It then appears that we are among the privileged."* —Helen Keller

Practice:

BE AWARE AND EMBRACE THE FEELING

As you have learned with the other compost seeds, the first step is to be aware of jealousy when it arises. By noticing the feeling and your reaction, you gain a clue to what is happening in the present moment. Clearly when jealousy arises it indicates that we believe our own personal needs are not being met. Instead of going outside of yourself to meet those needs, turn inside and water the seeds that nurture true love—loving-kindness, compassion, joy and equanimity.

Mindful breathing

Learning to embrace any feeling starts with the awareness of our breathing. A simple in-breath and out-breath will offer relief right away. Combine your breathing with a mindful walk, and the waves of jealousy will subside.

> *Breathing in, I feel the waves of jealousy.*
> *Breathing out, I release this feeling.*

Be aware that love begins with you

There is only one alternative to jealousy—self value or self love. If you are unable to love yourself, it will be challenging to receive love from others. Watering your positive seeds, you will discover your own worth. If you are truly practicing loving-kindness, you will realize that it begins with an unconditional love and acceptance of self.

Practice gratitude and generosity

As we explored in earlier chapters, gratitude and generosity are two seeds that nourish others and ourselves. By watering these seeds, we place the attention on others. Our ego subsides when we are present and able to observe the moment and be grateful for each breath, each person, and the gifts that continue to bless our being. In another breath, we are able to give what we have to others, and thus expand their lives through our gifts.

Communicate

The practice of deep listening in itself may offer insights for others, especially for those with whom we have experienced jealousy. Inviting a friend for tea may well begin the healing process. During your time together, focus on listening to the other to gain understanding. With loving-speech and a stable emotional balance, express your hurt and describe your feelings. Find ways to explain how you are feeling when he or she behaves in a certain way, for example, "When you frequently check your cell phone when we are together, I feel less important than whoever else might be calling." If your relationship is valuable to you both, you can expect them to become more aware of their behavior. The ultimate goal is for each to ask, "How can I best love you?"

SHARE YOUR FEELINGS

Is someone behaving in a way that prompts you to feel jealous? Simply letting them know can often help the problem. If the other person cares for you, they will want to change a behavior that brings you pain. Being aware of your feelings is the first step in healing a relationship as well as coping with relationships you cannot change.

EXPLORE YOUR JEALOUS FEELINGS

Through the practice of mindfulness, we can develop a deeper understanding of the source of the seed of jealousy within us. Looking deeply, consider: Why am I jealous in this situation or with this individual? What does another have that I covet? Why should I have it and not them? Does being jealous help me get what I want? Would I be happier if I had it? Why am I not happy that another has this? Such deep, rich questioning helps us gain understanding of the true nature of jealousy in our lives. The answers can offer us the opportunity to uncover the seed of jealousy and bring it to the light of transformation.

Water the Seed of Love.

Now is the time to recall the seeds of love that need to be watered for true love to blossom—loving-kindness, compassion, joy and equanimity. If we truly want the best for another, we celebrate their success and feel happy for them. In watering the seed of compassion, any suffering that may occur during experiences of jealousy can become a gift to strengthen the quality of our compassion.

Watering the seed of joy, I ultimately realize that another's joy will also bring delight to me. When I offer myself as refuge and provide freedom for others, I am practicing equanimity and thus both parties benefit and grow.

Mantras:
- Jealousy asks me to focus on being grateful for what I have.
- I am reminded to remember that I am enough.
- Jealousy directs me to practice loving-kindness and compassion for myself.

CHAPTER 19

Doubt

"If the Sun and Moon should ever doubt, they'd immediately go out." —William Blake

Mother Teresa was one of the most revered people of the 20th century, so it was a great surprise when, nearly ten years after her death, a collection of her personal writings revealed that in the midst of her absolute conviction that she was serving God, this amazing woman of faith had doubts, debilitating doubts about her faith and even the existence of the God she served. Doubt is indeed a universal experience and familiar to each of us. The seeds of doubt are often 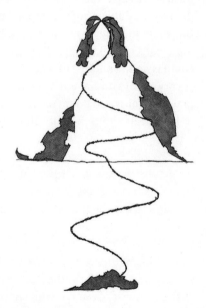 buried so deep within our consciousness that those around us would be surprised to know they even exist.

Many Faces of Doubt

Doubt has many disguises: uncertainty, indecision, hesitation, skepticism, confusion, and lack of conviction, to name a few. A close relative of doubt is inadequacy, which breeds feelings of incompetence, incapability, unfitness, ineffectiveness, impotence, powerlessness, inferiority and mediocrity.

Doubt also has its virtues. Healthy questioning is the basis of all scientific and educational pursuits. From a Christian perspective doubts lead to questioning which often leads to solutions. It is, after all, understandable that we are confused when faced with the complex ideologies faith can present. When the apostle Peter followed Jesus to walk on water, he set out onto the waves, then quickly began to sink as doubts arose. Jesus reached out his hand to support Peter and responded, "O you of little faith, why did you doubt?" Buddhists are encouraged not to be bound to any doctrine, theory, or ideology, including Buddhist ones; questioning is a guiding means of looking deeply and of developing understanding and compassion. Buddhists learn that faith means not accepting any theory until you have discovered its value in your own life and practice. Faith and doubt are inseparable. The gift of doubt is a call to look deeper into the faith that you hold.

> *"We can let the circumstances of our lives harden us so that we become increasingly resentful and afraid, or we can let them soften us and make us kinder and more open to what scares us. We always have this choice. Faith is being open to what scares us."*
>
> ——*Pema Chodron*

Looking at the seed of doubt and how it arises can offer insights, serving as a gateway to the deeper issues that may be germinating in the compost of our consciousness. Examining doubt in this way allows us to develop a healthy self-image and practice loving-kindness to generate insights about ourselves, thereby preparing us to do the same in relationships with others.

Personally, writing about the seed of doubt offered me a deeper understanding of an experience in my own life—an experience that, until now, had been hidden in the compost of a life that for the most part has been happy and successful. It is probably safe to say that, given the advances in medicine and psychology over the last several years, I would most likely have been diagnosed with what is now known as ADHD (Attention Deficit Hyperactivity Disorder) in elementary school.

Without access to today's knowledge of this disorder, my teachers were naturally confused about how best to support my learning experiences. Often my hyperactivity was seen as a behavioral issue, and I was disciplined accordingly. In the fourth grade, I was placed in what the teacher named "the rotten apple row" designated for students the teacher labeled "trouble-makers." This embarrassment and shame served to plant seeds of doubt within my store consciousness that continue to surface at various times in my life. I have often worked harder to prove myself, to show the world that I was somebody—clearly ego-based responses. The seeds of doubt were buried deeply, and I repeatedly watered this seed in my life until it became a mental formation or story of inadequacy. I have often been my own worst critic, judging myself as being not quite enough. Inadequacy, like any mental formation, takes shape over the years by allowing thoughts and feelings to become reality when in fact the majority of them are based on FEAR, or False Evidence Appearing Real.

> *"I am larger and better than I thought. I did not think I held so much goodness."* —Walt Whitman

When we can look deeply at the seeds of doubt within us, we are able to free ourselves from the stories that keep them buried in the soil of our consciousness. We can discover the wisdom they offer and transform them into acts of loving-kindness, compassion and, at times, even forgiveness. The teacher who created the "rotten apple row" was not aware of the seeds she was planting in her students. She may have even believed that these youngsters would be better for her disciplinary efforts. Like Mother Teresa, the teacher may have had doubts. Both carried on in their work and continued to hope that some day the faith they professed would be validated and they would see the results they anticipated.

Doubt and Relationships

The impact of doubt can be seen in all relationships. If a parent is constantly watering the seed of doubt, their children will be more likely to question themselves, be uncertain about their decisions, and be confused or lack conviction. On the other hand, when a parent acts with strength and confidence, their children are more likely to respond in similar ways.

When I doubt myself, I can set into motion feelings of insecurity within my partner or family network. Individuals who have experienced separation and or divorce often water the seeds of doubt with "Am I okay? Am I lovable? Will anyone ever love me again?" Instead of watering the seed of love, individuals in unhealthy or unhappy relationships are more likely to allow their thoughts to remain in the compost of their consciousness in doubt, fear and anger.

You Are Enough

Doubt may also cause us to question life in general. Lacking confidence or courage to move forward or challenge our doubts may lead us to question our life goals, hopes and dreams. We may question our achievements, accomplishments and even our spiritual practice. Doubt keeps us stuck in place, unable to grow, to reach, to change. A hallmark of doubt is often the feeling of not being "enough."

In addition, doubt sets up a belief within us that we need to have more and more to be happy. If we saw ourselves as already adequate, fulfilled and happy with what we have, we would be watering the seed of gratitude instead of the seed of doubt. In an excerpt from her poem "Knowing We Have Enough," Sister Annabel, a monastic in the Thich Nhat Hanh community, illustrates this concept:

> *"This is enough, I know it well.*
> *This is enough, I don't need more.*
> *The call of the bird in the bleak gray sky."*

The seed of gratitude can transform our doubts and encourage the seed of love to flourish within us, teaching us to have a strong self image as we walk in equanimity with others. A friend recently gave me the gift of seeing the possibility of transforming the "rotten apple row" experience with her gentle suggestion that, "You will heal this when you can turn the rotten apple row into the 'golden apple row'" and explore the gifts that grew from the difficult experience. Her suggestion helped me transform the seed of doubt to a seed of gratitude.

Practice:

NAME YOUR DEMONS

As with fear, learn to name your doubt demons—"Hello, Doubt. Are you back to see me again? Shall we have tea?" As with all the seeds of compost, resisting any of them only serves to bury them deeper in the soil of our consciousness.

> *Breathing in, I am aware of my doubt(s).*
> *Breathing out, I look deeply at its source.*

Naming our doubts or inadequacies offers us an opportunity to witness how they influence our body, feelings, perceptions or the story that we are creating. How long are we willing to allow the seed of doubt to remain in our mind consciousness? Learning to name and face the demon minimizes its long-term influence.

"When we become skillful at naming our experience, we discover an amazing truth. We find that no state of mind, no feeling, no emotion actually lasts more than fifteen or thirty seconds before it's replaced by some other one." —Jack Kornfield

INVESTIGATE YOUR "DOUBT STORY"

What is the story or mental formation created around your doubts? Where did this doubt come from? How might you be able to change the focus and bring your awareness back to watering seeds that are more nurturing and representative of your higher values? How might you change the discourse from doubt to faith—faith in yourself, others and the values that provided true love in yourself and your relationships?

PRACTICE THE PYGMALION EFFECT

The myth of Pygmalion offers a wonderful metaphor for transforming the seed of doubt. The sculptor Pygmalion created a statue that, to him, represented the most beautiful woman in the world. As the story goes, he falls in love with his creation. Through his prayers, she comes to life, and they lived happily ever after. The "Pygmalion Effect," as it is known, offers a wonderful antidote to doubt. When we project onto another our beliefs and expectations for their highest good, we water seeds in them that can only blossom into beautiful flowers. Seeing the deeper beauty in ourselves and others is a powerful way to transform deep-seated feelings of doubt and inadequacy.

"If we have doubt in our heart we cannot practice. We have to resolve this doubt by looking deeply, by going to that person or writing them, asking our teacher, our brother, our sister to shine light on us so we can overcome this doubt." —Thich Nhat Hanh

Mantras:

- When doubt arises, I shine a light to discover the source.
- Today, I look for the positive qualities in everyone I meet.
- When experiencing doubt, I practice gratitude.
- I have enough and I am enough.

Conclusion

CHAPTER 20

Creating a Legacy as a Master Gardener: Tending Your Inner Garden

"Inside every one of us is a garden, and every practitioner has to go back to their garden and take care of it. Maybe in the past, you left it untended for a long time. You should know exactly what is going on in your own garden, and try to put everything in order. Restore the beauty; restore the harmony in your garden. If it is well tended, many people will enjoy your garden. " — *Thich Nhat Hanh*

Throughout these chapters, you have had the opportunity to tour the garden of your consciousness, learning to look deeply to explore the nature of your garden, seed by seed. Now, accept this invitation to take time to understand the story of how your garden was created and watered. Notice the flowers and lush vegetation. See where weeds have sprung up or soil has gone barren. You now know that, using mindfulness as your guide, you can create a new story by tilling the soil of your consciousness, watering the seeds of love, and transforming the seeds of suffering.

Who are the gardeners in your life—known and unknown—who have made your life possible? Begin with your ancestors, your parents, family, friends and colleagues, as well as individuals who perhaps never knew they had touched your mind and heart in some significant way. Next, find a quiet place and give yourself the space and time to stop and reflect on those who helped cultivate, fertilize, nurture, and plant the garden of your life.

Who were your "master gardeners"—those who often thought more about you than themselves? You now recognize them as the ones who most often watered the seeds of loving-kindness, compassion, joy and equanimity. How did they tend to your life? Your joy and happiness today were watered by the gardeners who were blessed with an abundance of those seeds in their own gardens. When these primary seeds were watered, you discovered the best ways to create the understanding necessary to know how best to love yourself and others.

Who were the gardeners who knew the skills needed to nurture the qualities of understanding and intimacy that supported your well-being and happiness? Offer appreciation for those who exemplified the qualities of deep listening, loving speech, gratitude and generosity. They helped you build the foundation of loving communication, the soil of connection and the language of the heart. Recognize that no matter when these seeds were watered in you, they are still and will always be in the garden of your consciousness. Like all seeds they await the ideal conditions to blossom and grow deeper in your awareness to influence your being in the world.

Using mindfulness as your guide, begin to till the soil and recognize the seeds of compost that are alive in your consciousness. Who were the gardeners in your life who contributed to your suffering or unhappiness in life by watering the seeds of fear, anger, jealousy and doubt? Often such gardeners were not aware or mindful of their actions—they were unintentionally watering in you the seeds of their own suffering. As these people come to mind, you may naturally project your fear and anger onto them.

However, as you meditate from your quiet space, may you come to recognize that, in most cases, under the circumstances, these gardeners did their best, given the nature and conditions of their own gardens. May you discover that, through forgiveness and letting go, you will be less likely to water these seeds in yourself and in those you love. As you continue to transform the seeds of suffering, your ability to love yourself and others will blossom and flourish—in your garden and theirs.

Finally, learn to walk through the garden of your consciousness in a state of profound gratitude:

- for yourself, the gardener
- for individuals who have watered both the seeds of love and the seeds of compost
- for each experience of love and joy whose blessings are easily welcomed and embraced
- for each challenging life experience that offers you an unseen gift of opportunity if you choose to let go of bitterness or resentment

In continually offering yourself the time and space to stop and mindfully reflect on your life story, you will discover that watering the seeds of love becomes your most exciting and rewarding life practice.

Master Gardening Guidelines

As you move forward in life with your new awareness of your role as a Master Gardener, you will need to stop now and then to review the lessons you've learned until practice becomes second nature. These review guidelines are also a simple way to share with others the basics of your new practice, because others are sure to notice the changes in you as you tend to your garden and tend also to theirs. Most of all, these guidelines provide a touchstone for those times emotions arise and you need a quick reminder of the many tools at your disposal as the Master Gardener of your life:

Practice mindfulness by stopping, calming and looking deeply at what is happening now, in the present moment. By learning to stop, you let go of the past and future as you focus on what is immediately present— your breath, a person, a task. You discover that place of calming that resides within your mind and body. By looking deeply, you establish your ability to see the connection between what is taking place in the present moment and what has happened in the past—the seeds that were watered.

Be aware of what is going on in your body, what you are feeling, what you are thinking and perceiving, what story you are telling yourself, and how this is influencing the garden of your consciousness. Every moment, your body is teaching you what is happening in the present. By exploring messages from your body, your thoughts and feelings as they arise, you deepen your connection with the present moment. These influences create a story or mental formation that affect your consciousness.

Create an imaginary door between your mind consciousness and store consciousness. A healthy garden needs good filtration and circulation between the flowers and the earth. Similarly, by keeping this imaginary door open, you are creating the proper aeration so that the seeds can easily circulate between both levels of the garden of your consciousness. This positive circulation between all the seeds— seeds of compost and seeds of love—supports the positive mental and physical well-being of the garden. In this way, we flow into each situation being free to experience our feelings without resisting them or dwelling on them.

Embrace all seeds and avoid pushing them away—they are all teachers and opportunities for growth. Welcoming each seed as it arises is a profound opportunity and perhaps the best method for gaining insights about what is really unfolding in us in each moment.

Learn how to nurture or water the proper seeds—the seeds of love. Through understanding others, you have learned which seeds need the most attention. You know that it is essential to water loving-kindness, compassion, joy and equanimity on a daily basis. You further realize that, through deep listening and loving speech, you are discovering other seeds that may need attention—and you may find new ways to express your love. You also know that when you express gratitude and generosity, you are less concerned about self and truly free to water the seeds of love in others.

press gratitude and generosity, you are less concerned about self and truly free to water the seeds of love in others.

Learn how to weed out and transform the negative seeds—the seeds of suffering. As the seeds of suffering arise—fear, anger, jealousy and doubt—you are now willing to look at them as core seeds. They arise in nearly every circumstance in which there is anxiety, confusion and stress. Remember that all seeds "inter-are." They synergistically connect and feed each other like compost in healthy soil. When you experience doubt, fear and anger are likely hiding out in the weeds waiting to emerge. As you experience jealousy, notice that anger may also be present. Learn to look deeply, beyond what is obvious to what may be the core of your reaction.

Become aware of the concept of "indicator" seeds. This term was coined from the term "indicator species," whose presence in nature reflects a specific environmental condition. For example, when a person is truly able to listen deeply, they create an environment in which they are more likely to generate loving speech and equanimity. No one seed stands alone. In addition, the absence of fear, anger and doubt is a reminder that you are watering the positive seeds. The absence of pain allows you to focus on what is beautiful in that moment.

Learn to selectively water. The song of love is knowing which seeds to water and when to nourish those qualities in those we love. When we have true love in our relationships, we have understanding. If a flower is wilting, doubt may be present. Take a moment to refresh the flower. Reminding others of their gifts of kindness and compassion may be all that is needed.

Surround yourself with spiritual friends who are capable of watering the best seeds in you and you in them. Often, the seeds within you are best perceived through your interaction with friends who are able see what you cannot. Friends who can shine light and share with loving speech are a rare gift. They offer a true reflection and the deepest hope for transformation and growth.

Ancient wisdom reminds us that even a blade of grass needs encouragement, so how much more do the people in our lives need us to whisper words of inspiration into their lives? Remember, "You are precious. You can do it. Your birth has been a gift. Grow." Do you feel more encouraged? Now imagine the look on your loved one's face when you say, "You are perfect as you are. You are such a joy. I am here for you. Thank you for being in my life."

Make a commitment to whisper to others, "You are enough, just as you are." If you respond to that calling, your life and the lives you touch will continue to grow as beautiful gardens. You, as the Master Gardener, have learned that the seeds of love are within you. May you wake up to the beauty within you so that your life will be a legacy, and those around you will remember you in loving ways forever.

Bibliography

Altman, Donald. *Living Kindness*. Makawao, Maui: Inner Ocean Publishing, Inc., 2003.

Barks, Coleman and John Moyne. *Rumi: The Book of Love: Poems of Ecstasy and Longing*. New York: HarperCollins Publishers Inc., 2003.

Benson, Herbert. *Beyond the Relaxation Response: How to Harness the Healing Power*. New York: HarperCollins Publishers Limited, 1985.

Borysenko, Joan. *Inner Peace for Busy People: Simple Strategies for Transforming your Life*. Carlsbad, California: Hayhouse, 2001.

Breathnacht, Sarah Ban. *Simple Abundance*. New York: Werner Books, 1995.

Brach, Tara. *Radical Acceptance: Embracing Your Life with the Heart of a Buddha*. New York: Bantam, 2003.

Braza, Jerry. *Moment by Moment: The Art and Practice of Mindfulness*. Rutland, VT: Tuttle Publishing, 1997.

Dalai Lama and Howard Cutler. *The Art of Happiness*. New York: Riverhead Books, 1998.

Chodron, Pema. *The Places That Scare You: A Guide to Fearlessness in Difficult Times*. Boston: Shambahla Publications, 2001.

Dang Nghiem, Sister. *Healing: A Woman's Journey from Doctor to Nun*. Berkeley: Parallax Press, 2010.

Dass, Ram. *Be Love Now: The Path of the Heart*. New York: Harper Collins, 2010.

Dyer, Wayne. *There's a Spiritual Solution to Every Problem*. New York: Harper Collins, 2001.

Ferrucci, Piero. *The Power of Kindness: The Unexpected Benefits of Leading a Compassionate Life*. Boston: Shambahla Publications, 2007.

Frankl, Viktor. *Man's Search for Meaning: An Introduction to Logotherapy*, Boston: Beacon Press, 2004.

Fronsdal, Gil. *A Monastery Within: Tales from the Buddhist Path*. California: Tranquil Books, 2010.

Gottman, John. *Seven Principles for Making Marriage Work*. New York: Crown Publishers, 2000.

Hanh, Thich Nhat. *Anger: Wisdom for Cooling the Flames*. New York: Riverhead Books, 2001.

Hanh, Thich Nhat. *Buddha Mind, Buddha Body: Walking Toward Enlightenment*. Berkeley: Parallax Press, 2007.

Hanh, Thich Nhat. *Creating True Peace: Ending Violence in Yourself, Your Family, Your Community, and the World.* New York: Free Press, 2003.

Hanh, Thich Nhat. *Happiness: Essential Mindfulness Practices*. Berkeley: Parallax Press, 2009.

Hanh, Thich Nhat. *The Heart of the Buddha's Teaching*. Berkeley: Parallax Press, 1998.

Hanh, Thich Nhat. *No Death, No Fear: Comforting Wisdom for Life.* New York: Riverhead Books, 2002.

Hanh, Thich Nhat. *Nothing to Do Nowhere to Go: Waking Up to Who You Are*. Berkeley: Parallax Press, 2007.

Hanh, Thich Nhat. *Peace is Every Breath: A Practice for Our Busy Lives*. New York: Harper Collins, 2011.

Hanh, Thich Nhat. *Reconciliation: Healing the Inner Child*. Berkeley: Parallax Press, 2010.

Hanh, Thich Nhat and Lilian Cheung. *Savor: Mindful Eating, Mindful Life*. New York: Harper One, 2010.

Hanh, Thich Nhat. *Taming the Tiger Within*. New York, Riverhead Books, 2005.

Hanh, Thich Nhat. *Teaching on Love*. Berkeley: Parallax Press, 1997.

Hanh, Thich Nhat. *Transformation at the Base*. Berkeley: Parallax Press, 2001.

Hanh, Thich Nhat. *True Love: A Practice for Awakening the Heart*. Boston: Shambhala, 2004.

Hanh, Thich Nhat. *True Love*. Boston: Shambhala Publications, 1997.

Hanh, Thich Nhat. *You Are Here: Discovering the Magic of the Present Moment*. Boston: Shambhala Publications, 2009.

Hanson, Rick. *Buddha's Brain: The Practical Neuroscience of Happiness, Love and Wisdom*. Oakland: New Harbinger, 2009.

Jampolsky, Gerald. *Love is Letting Go of Fear*. Milbrae, California: Celestial Arts, 1979.

Kabat-Zinn, Jon. *Coming to Our Senses: Healing Ourselves and the World Through Mindfulness*. New York: Hyperion, 2005.

Kornfield, Jack. *A Path with Heart: a Guide Through the Perils and Promises of a Spiritual Life*. New York: Bantam, 1993.

Kornfield, Jack. *The Buddha is Still Teaching: Cotemporary Buddhist Wisdom*. Boston: Shambhala, 2010.

Kornfield, Jack. *The Wise Heart: a Guide to the Universal Teachings of Buddhist Psychology*. New York: Bantam, 2008.

Larkin, Geri. Plant Seed, *Pull Weed: Nurturing the Garden of Your Life*. New York: Harper One, 2008.

Martin, William. *The Couple's Tao Te Ching*. New York: Marlow and Company, 2000.

McClelland, David and others. "The Effects of Motivational Arousal through Films on Salivary Immunoglobulin A." Psychology and Health, Issue 2,Vol. 2, 1988: 31-52.

Miller, Alice and Andrew Jenkins. *The Body Never Lies: The Lingering Effects of Hurtful Parenting*. New York: W. W. Norton & Company, 2006.

Moore, Thomas. *Soul Mates: Honoring the Mystery of Love and Relationship*. New York. Harper Perennial, 1994.

Mother Teresa. *The Joy in Loving: A Guide to Daily Living*. Berkeley: Penguin, 2000

Muller, Wayne. *How Then Shall We Live?: Four Simple Questions That Reveal the Beauty and Meaning Of Our Lives*. New York: Bantam, 1996.

Nouwen, Henri. *Sabbatical Journey: The Diary of His Final Years*. Chestnut Ridge, NY: The Crossroads Publishing, 2000.

Norris, Gunilla. *A Mystic Garden: Working with Soil, Attending to Soul,* New York: Bluebridge, 2006.

O'Donohue, John. *Anam Cara: A Book of Celtic Wisdom*. New York: Harper Collins, 1998.

O'Donohue, John. *Beauty: Rediscovering The True Sources of Compassion, Serenity, and Hope*. New York: Harper, 2004.

Pennington, Bail. *Centering Prayer*. Clearwater, Florida: Sea Shell Books, 1982.

Pierce, Brian J. *We Walk the Path Together: Learning from Thich Nhat Hanh and Meister Eckhart*. Maryknoll, New York: Orbis Books, 2005.

Remen, Rachel Naomi. *Kitchen Table Wisdom*. New York: Riverbend, 1996.

Ricard, Matthieu. *Happiness: A Guide to Developing Life's Most Important Skill*. New York: Little Brown and Company, 2006.

Ricio, David. *How to Be an Adult in Relationships: The Five Keys to Mindful Loving*. Boston: Shambhala Publications, 2002.

Rosenberg, Marshall. *Nonviolent Communication: A Language of Compassion*.Encinitas, California: Puddle Dancer Press, 1999.

Rowe, Peggy and Larry Ward. *Love's Garden*. Berkeley: Parallax Press, 2007.

Satir, Virginia. *Making Contact*. Berkeley: Celestial Arts. 1976

Servan-Schreiber, David. *Anti Cancer: A New Way of Life*. New York: Viking, 2009.

Shafir, Rebecca. *The Zen of Listening: Mindful Communication in the Age of Distraction*. Wheaton, Illinois: Theosophical Publishing, 2000.

Shunryu, Suzuki, *Zen Mind Beginner's Mind*. New York: Weatherhill, 1970.

Tolle, Eckhart. *A New Earth: Awakening to Your Life's Purpose*. New York: Penguin, 2006.

Tolle, Eckhart. *The Power of Now: A Guide to Spiritual Enlightenment*. Novato: The New World Library, 1999.

Vardey, Lucinda and John Dallla Costa. *Being Generous: The Art of Right Living*. Canada: Vintage, 2008.

Wiesel, Elie. *Night*. New York: Hot, Rinehart and Winston, 1999.

Zajonc, Arthur. *Meditation as Contemplative Inquiry*. Herndon, VA: Lindisfarne Books, 2009.

In Gratitude....

Happiness is having a teacher, a partner, family, friends, and a practice that "waters *the seeds of love.*" I first bow to my teacher—Zen Master Thich Nhat Hanh. If it were not for his teachings and inspiration, this book would not have manifested. I am especially grateful for his generous endorsement in his foreword, which eloquently expresses the true meaning found in this book. I bow deeply to all my other teachers and especially Ram Dass and Jack Kornfield, who were my first meditation teachers and ignited in me a passion to look deeply and live in the present moment.

I offer gratitude to my ancestors, parents and brothers who watered the seeds of love in me. I extend my deepest love and appreciation for my wife and partner of more than thirty years, Kathleen, whose support and belief in me was unwavering during this process. She offered both editorial insights and gentle reminders that practicing these principles are just as important as writing about them. The best part of this journey has been the opportunity for us to look deeply at the seeds that we have watered in our life together. In Kathleen, I have discovered that we all need a person who believes in us and sings our song when we forget. Thank you, Kathleen, for watering the "seeds of love" in me—a gift that keeps giving and a song that keeps singing.

I wish to honor my son and daughter, Mark and Andrea. I am so proud of who you are and who you are becoming. Together we continue to water the seeds of love, while nurturing these qualities in my two beloved grandsons, Andrew and Daniel.

I offer a special bow to my Kalyna Mitra (spiritual friends) in the worldwide Thich Nhat Hahn community who so beautifully model and practice mindfulness and loving-kindness. In addition, I honor a stream of teachers including the monastics in Plum Village community and those at the Trappist Abbey in Lafayette, Oregon, whose insights and way of being have become a catalyst and reminder to live a more authentic life.

I have been blessed to have the editorial support of Rebecca Brant, who always seemed to understand just what I was trying to say and somehow made the words more beautiful through her reflections, wisdom, and spiritual insights. She helped me create a book that provides insights from a variety of wisdom traditions with love as the foundation.

I am most fortunate for the ongoing support of Tuttle Publishing, who also published my first book, *Moment by Moment: The Art and Practice of Mindfulness*. It has been a pleasure to have the support of the entire Tuttle team, and I am especially grateful for the insightful editing and reflections offered by editor Terri Jadick. In gentle and caring ways, she asked the hard questions, which required me to look deeply and not lose sight of the bigger picture. Her editing offered an important objective and sensitive overview to help the readers develop the confidence needed to apply this material to their lives.

During my years in academia, I was privileged to work with hundreds of students who offered insights, stories, challenges and opportunities to apply the concepts in this book. I have also been blessed to have a number of dear friends who shined light on this book during the review process. Their insights and support allowed me to affirm the clarity and personal relevance of this message.

It is important to begin any journey with confidence and support—Nadene LeCheminant's caring support helped me craft the proposal that resulted in this book. I was also fortunate to have a reading panel of spiritual friends who offered guidance and support on this journey: Charles Busch, Robert Brevoort, Arthur Davis, Denise Segor, Ann Marie Skierski, Michael Donovan, Peggy Lindquist, Jessica Henderson, Werner Brandt, Bob Welsh, Joe Spaeder, Carol Mitchell, Ken Oefelein, Larry Sipe, Alice Phalan, Martin Kopf, Dan

Lassila, Randall Burton, Robert Hautala, David Steinberg, Peter Cutler and Nacho Cordova. I value the support of Ron Glaus and Gerald Nathan, who offered their friendship, wisdom and psychological insights. I truly appreciate the dharma insights from teachers and friends on the path—Eileen Kierra, Richard Brady and Bill Menza and a variety of reviewers whose names are mentioned in this book or on my website.

Special thanks to my friends Rita Thomas and Jim McBride, who graciously offered me a writing sanctuary, affectionately known as "The Barn," with its magnificent views and quietude.

Finally, I am grateful for the beautiful illustrations created by artist, illustrator, teacher and writer Linda McGill. If you look deeply, you will see in each seed the qualities it represents. In these illustrations the energy of the seeds is expanded, offering an image for personal self-awareness and growth. The illustrations are a reflection of Linda's loving spirit and insights. These seeds and flowers are an ongoing invitation for you to explore what seeds you are watering and what kind of flower you are becoming today. For those who are interested in looking deeply at their own journey of self-discovery illuminated through art, she can be reached through her website at www.wyndvisions.com

I would love to hear about how you, the reader, are doing as you water the seeds of love in your life. You can contact me through my website: www.wateringtheseedsoflove.com.

Short anecdotes would be appreciated to demonstrate how these concepts are being applied to the relationships in your life. With your permission these stories will be posted on my website.

Enjoy the journey of becoming a Master Gardener!

THAT WHICH WE NURTURE IN OURSELVES
IS THAT WHICH WE BECOME.